Celebrate
the Feasts
of the Lord

*The Christian Heritage of
the Sacred Jewish Festivals*

William W. Francis

Foreword by Roger J. Green

Crest Books

Salvation Army National Publications
615 Slaters Lane
Alexandria, Virginia 22313

Endorsements

Every Christian has Jewish biblical roots. Jesus was a Jew and the original first century church was totally Jewish, both deeply committed to the Old Testament Scriptures. William Francis has written a valuable book that informs the church of an often neglected aspect of its Hebraic heritage—the historical and spiritual significance of the biblical feasts. The author is a veteran traveler to the Holy Land and an astute student of Jewish life and culture. In this work, William Francis effectively guides his readers to a greater understanding of how the Old Testament links to the New. By unfolding the calendar of biblical feasts he clearly demonstrates their profound importance—past, present and future—within the life of the church. I am delighted to recommend this work.

—Dr. Marvin R. Wilson
Professor of Biblical and Theological Studies
Gordon College, Wenham, Massachusetts

Celebrate the Feasts of the Lord is a marvelous achievement. William Francis has written a wonderful book that provides the reader with a deep appreciation of the Old Testament feasts ordained by God and their relevance to the life and ministry of our Lord and Savior, Jesus Christ. His thorough handling of each feast in relation to its relevance to contemporary life provides us with a context in which to appreciate the Jewish roots of the Christian faith and to better appreciate the spiritual high points in the calendar for our Jewish friends and colleagues. *Celebrate the Feasts of the Lord* is a must for mature and maturing Christians and Jews who wish to appreciate the common ground of a shared heritage of faith.

—Dr. Jonathan S. Raymond
Senior Vice President for Academic Affairs
Greenville College, Greenville, Illinois

Celebrate the Feasts of the Lord is a worthy successor to the author's previous work, *The Stones Cry Out*. His numerous visits to Israel and his precise probing as a prospector for gems of cultural insight to the Hebraic heritage of the church distinguish William W. Francis as a preeminent voice among contemporary authorities on the Holy Land. As you begin to turn the pages of this scholarly, devotional book, you will soon realize that you are seated at the banquet table, enjoying the Feasts of the Lord.

—Lt. Colonel William D. MacLean, Literary Secretary
USA Eastern Territory, West Nyack, New York

Celebrate the Feasts of the Lord is a valuable and informative book which combines a lucid style and careful scholarship without the intrusion of multiple citations and footnotes. The reader first learns about each feast's origin, then its meaning and practice among the Jews, and finally its significance for Christians. These Hebrew holy days make it clear that community is central to celebration and that coming together in joyful worship nourishes our souls, our social relationships and, on occasion, our bodies. Finally, the value of the volume is enhanced by a helpful bibliography of some two dozen items for those wishing to explore these Old Testament Feasts of the Lord in greater depth and detail.

—Dr. Daniel R. Chamberlain, President
Houghton College, Houghton, New York

We Jews observe the Sabbath and festivals today as we have since biblical times. They invest our lives with spirituality and godliness. The challenge for Christians is to find meaning in biblical rituals that seem consigned to a bygone era and a foreign culture. My friend, William Francis, offers an interpretation of the festivals that makes them central to Christian life. While our understanding of the practices and their meanings differ substantially, I applaud the revival of a God–given lifestyle among all people of faith.

—Rabbi Judah Kogen
Congregation Sons of Israel, Suffern, New York

Also by William W. Francis
The Stones Cry Out. New York: The Salvation Army
(USA Eastern Territory), 1993.

Published by Crest Books, The Salvation Army National Publications,
615 Slaters Lane, Alexandria, VA 22313
(703) 684-5500 • Fax: (703) 684-5539

Printed in the United States of America.

ISBN: 0-9657601-2-X

Chapters 1-9 originally were published in a twelve–part series in the USA *War
Cry* (ISSN 0043-0234). The first article appeared in the January 7, 1995 issue,
and the last in June 24, 1995.

Unless otherwise indicated, Scripture quotations are taken from the New International Version of the Bible, copyright © 1973, 1978, 1984 by the International Bible Society. Published by Zondervan Bible Publishers. All rights reserved. Used by permission.

Other Scripture quotations are identified as KJV (King James Version), RSV
(Revised Standard Version) or NEB (New English Bible).

Drawings of *Herod the Great's Temple Mount* (color pages) and *Jerusalem in
30 A.D.* (page 94) by Leen Ritmeyer.

The Meaning of the Jewish Holy Days chart (page 128) from *Israel's Holy Days*
by Daniel Fuchs. Used by permission of Loizeaux Brothers, Inc., Neptune, New
Jersey.

Line drawings of *Jerusalem in Jesus' Day* (page 7), *Herodian Palestine* (page
36) and the *Second Temple* (page 81) taken from *The Outpouring* by Elwood
McQuaid, © copyright The Friends of Israel Gospel Ministry, Inc., Bellmawr,
NJ. Used by permission.

Publication approved by USA Eastern Territory Literary Council (Colonel Israel L. Gaither, Chairman; Lt. Colonel William D. MacLean, Secretary).

Layout and design by Marlene Chase and Timothy Clark.

Dedication

This book is dedicated to my father and mother, Harold and Marjorie Francis—devoted, faithful, loving soldiers of Christ. They were sterling examples of Christian parents who taught the scriptures "diligently to [their] children" (Deuteronomy 6:7 RSV).

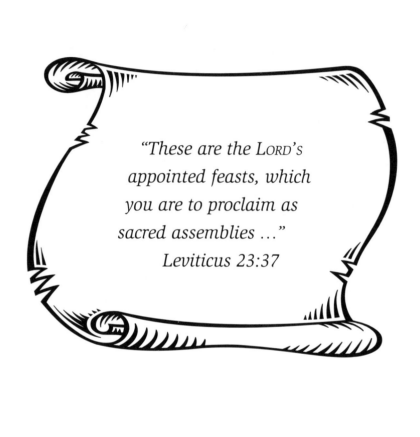

"These are the LORD's
appointed feasts, which
you are to proclaim as
sacred assemblies ..."
Leviticus 23:37

Contents

Acknowledgments

While thanking everyone by name who extended encouragement, assistance and prayer support is not possible, I am truly grateful to all those who prompted me to write this book. I am specifically indebted to the following family and friends:

My wife, Marilyn, and children, Billy, Susan and son-in-law, Nicholas, for their invaluable inspiration, affirming encouragement and abiding patience.

My friends and colleagues, Dr. Marvin R. Wilson, Dr. Jonathan S. Raymond, Dr. Daniel R. Chamberlain, Rabbi Judah Kogen and Lt. Colonel William D. MacLean for their insightful, meticulous scrutiny of the manuscript and generous endorsements.

Dr. Roger J. Green, chairperson of Biblical and Theological Studies at Gordon College, friend of four decades, for his enthusiastic encouragement and for providing the Foreword.

The former editor in chief of the USA *War Cry*, Colonel Henry Gariepy (R), for first suggesting the 12-part series in *The War Cry*, and the present editor in chief, Lt. Colonel Marlene Chase, for proposing that it be expanded to become the third offering of The Salvation Army National Book Publishing Plan.

The Eastern Territorial Literary Council, including territorial commander Commissioner Ronald G. Irwin and literary secretary Lt. Colonel William D. MacLean.

My secretaries, Carole Stollenwerk and Stephanie Elynich,

for their careful proofreading, handling of correspondence and project organization. Timothy Clark, who served as project manager for the National Publications and Literary Department, for his painstaking work on the index and layout.

Above all, I acknowledge the abiding love and grace of the Lord, who through the Holy Spirit, has promised to "guide [us] into all truth" (John 16:13).

Foreword

Christians too often ignore their own history. We have failed to recognize that the Old Testament was the Scripture of our Lord and the earliest Christians, and that the land of Israel was not only the place of the birth of Jesus but the place of his life and ministry, his death and resurrection. The Hebraic culture was the one in which our Lord was immersed, and the earliest Christians were Jewish. With his thorough knowledge of the Scriptures, the land of the Bible and Judaism, Lt. Colonel William Francis moves the reader through the intricate pathways of Old Testament passages with great skill. Because of his appreciation for Judaism, he brings our Hebraic heritage to light, and in doing so helps us to know ourselves.

He could certainly have chosen simpler Old Testament texts and themes to explain, but he chose, instead, the path of hard study and critical evaluation—primarily of Leviticus, a book which is not often the subject of the Sunday morning sermon. By his careful scholarship, historical analysis and sensitivity to the original meaning of the texts, he enlivens those passages for the Christian without in any way diminishing the historical, agricultural or sacrificial characteristics of the feasts. Lt. Colonel Francis applies the kind of interpretive skills to the text which model for all readers how the Word of God should be approached. His study of the messianic prophecies of the Old Testament are rooted in the New Testament texts which provide the full meaning of such prophecies, and thereby render this book an invaluable guide for how to interpret the feasts of the Lord specifically and how to interpret Scriptures generally.

One senses immediately the excitement of the author for this important subject, and so every reader of *Celebrate the Feasts of the Lord* will be moved along by the text in anticipation of the next word. This is especially true as the richer and deeper meaning of the feasts for Christians are available as "self–evident truths, without need to distort texts or misinterpret truths." All Christians will rejoice in this book because it is, in the last analysis, a book about our Lord Jesus Christ and the full range of his redemptive life and ministry.

Study guides have been provided at the end of each chapter, thereby assisting the reader in as comprehensive an understanding of this book as possible. This is further demonstration of the pastoral concern of Lt. Colonel Francis. His implied intention for this book is clear from beginning to end—to provide readers with a book which will be useful for study of the Scriptures, for sermon preparation and for personal devotions.

As one who has been privileged to read this book and to know the author, I am aware of the riches of the text which will unfold for every favored reader, and I share the anticipation of the author as this important book finds its way into the common life of the Church. May all who turn the pages of *Celebrate the Feasts of the Lord* find yourselves indeed feasting on this text with thanksgiving for the dedicated work of Lt. Colonel Francis and with joy for the ultimate message of the book.

Roger J. Green

Professor and Chair of Biblical and Theological Studies

Terrelle B. Crum Chair of Humanities

Gordon College, Wenham, Massachusetts

Leviticus 23

The Lord said to Moses, [2]"Speak to the Israelites and say to them: 'These are my appointed feasts, the appointed feasts of the Lord, which you are to proclaim as sacred assemblies.

The Sabbath

[3]"'There are six days when you may work, but the seventh day is a Sabbath of rest, a day of sacred assembly. You are not to do any work; wherever you live, it is a Sabbath to the Lord.

The Passover and Unleavened Bread

[4]"'These are the Lord's appointed feasts, the sacred assemblies you are to proclaim at their appointed times: [5]The Lord's Passover begins at twilight on the fourteenth day of the first month. [6]On the fifteenth day of that month the Lord's Feast of Unleavened Bread begins; for seven days you must eat bread made without yeast. [7]On the first day hold a sacred assembly and do no regular work. [8]For seven days present an offering made to the Lord by fire. And on the seventh day hold a sacred assembly and do no regular work.'"

Firstfruits

[9]The Lord said to Moses, [10]"Speak to the Israelites and say to them: 'When you enter the land I am going to give you and

you reap its harvest, bring to the priest a sheaf of the first grain you harvest. ¹¹He is to wave the sheaf before the Lᴏʀᴅ so it will be accepted on your behalf; the priest is to wave it on the day after the Sabbath. ¹²On the day you wave the sheaf, you must sacrifice as a burnt offering to the Lᴏʀᴅ a lamb a year old without defect, ¹³together with its grain offering of two-tenths of an ephah of fine flour mixed with oil—an of-fering made to the Lᴏʀᴅ by fire, a pleasing aroma—and its drink offering of a quarter of a hin of wine. ¹⁴You must not eat any bread, or roasted or new grain, until the very day you bring this offering to your God. This is to be a lasting ordi-nance for the generations to come, wherever you live.

Feast of Weeks
¹⁵"'From the day after the Sabbath, the day you brought the sheaf of the wave offering, count off seven full weeks. ¹⁶Count off fifty days up to the day after the seventh Sabbath, and then present an offering of new grain to the Lᴏʀᴅ. ¹⁷From wherever you live, bring two loaves made of two-tenths of an ephah of fine flour, baked with yeast, as a wave offering of firstfruits to the Lᴏʀᴅ. ¹⁸Present with this bread seven male lambs, each a year old and without defect, one young bull and two rams. They will be a burnt offering to the Lᴏʀᴅ, together with their grain offerings and drink offerings—an offering made by fire, an aroma pleasing to the Lᴏʀᴅ. ¹⁹Then sacrifice one male goat for a sin offering and two lambs, each a year old, for a fellowship offering. ²⁰The priest is to wave the two lambs before the Lᴏʀᴅ as a wave offering, together with the bread of the firstfruits. They are a sacred offering to the Lᴏʀᴅ for the priest. ²¹On that same day you are to proclaim a sacred assem-bly and do no regular work. This is to be a lasting ordinance

for the generations to come, wherever you live.

²²"'When you reap the harvest of your land, do not reap to the very edges of your field or gather the gleanings of your harvest. Leave them for the poor and the alien. I am the LORD your God.'"

Feast of Trumpets

²³The LORD said to Moses, ²⁴"Say to the Israelites: 'On the first day of the seventh month you are to have a day of rest, a sacred assembly commemorated with trumpet blasts. ²⁵Do no regular work, but present an offering made to the LORD by fire.'"

Day of Atonement

²⁶The LORD said to Moses, ²⁷ "The tenth day of this seventh month is the Day of Atonement. Hold a sacred assembly and deny yourselves, and present an offering made to the LORD by fire. ²⁸Do no work on that day, because it is the Day of Atonement, when atonement is made for you before the LORD your God. ²⁹Anyone who does not deny himself on that day must be cut off from his people. ³⁰I will destroy from among his people anyone who does any work on that day. ³¹You shall do no work at all. This is to be a lasting ordinance for the generations to come, wherever you live. ³²It is a sabbath of rest for you, and you must deny yourselves. From the evening of the ninth day of the month until the following evening you are to observe your sabbath."

Feast of Tabernacles

³³The LORD said to Moses, ³⁴"Say to the Israelites: 'On the fifteenth day of the seventh month the LORD's Feast of Taber-

nacles begins, and it lasts for seven days. [35]The first day is a sacred assembly; do no regular work. [36]For seven days present offerings made to the LORD by fire, and on the eighth day hold a sacred assembly and present an offering made to the LORD by fire. It is the closing assembly; do no regular work.

[37]("'These are the LORD's appointed feasts, which you are to proclaim as sacred assemblies for bringing offerings made to the LORD by fire—the burnt offerings and grain offerings, sacrifices and drink offerings required for each day. [38]These offerings are in addition to those for the Lord's Sabbaths and in addition to your gifts and whatever you have vowed and all the freewill offerings you give to the LORD.)

[39]"'So beginning with the fifteenth day of the seventh month, after you have gathered the crops of the land, celebrate the festival to the LORD for seven days; the first day is a day of rest, and the eighth day also is a day of rest. [40]On the first day you are to take choice fruit from the trees, and palm fronds, leafy branches and poplars, and rejoice before the LORD your God for seven days. [41]Celebrate this as a festival to the LORD for seven days each year. This is to be a lasting ordinance for the generations to come; celebrate it in the seventh month. [42]Live in booths for seven days: All native–born Israelites are to live in booths [43]so your descendants will know that I had the Israelites live in booths when I brought them out of Egypt. I am the LORD your God.'"

[44]So Moses announced to the Israelites the appointed feasts of the LORD.

Chapter 1

Feasts of the Lord

I have a precious gift in my treasury, said God to Moses: "Sabbath" is its name; go and tell Israel I wish to present it to them.

—Shabbath 10b

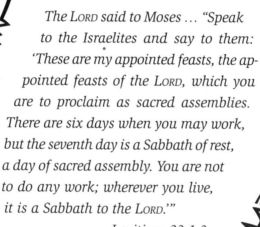

> The LORD said to Moses ... "Speak
> to the Israelites and say to them:
> 'These are my appointed feasts, the ap-
> pointed feasts of the LORD, which you
> are to proclaim as sacred assemblies.
> There are six days when you may work,
> but the seventh day is a Sabbath of rest,
> a day of sacred assembly. You are not
> to do any work; wherever you live,
> it is a Sabbath to the LORD.'"
> —Leviticus 23:1-3

$\mathcal{T}$he great truths of Scripture are celebrated and taught annually through the Jewish feasts. Some mistakenly consider the feasts to be ethnic celebrations holding little meaning for the follower of Christ. To the contrary, these sacred festivals provide a fascinating link to Christianity's historic and spiritual roots in Judaism.

Jesus actively participated in Jewish religious ritual from his early days when Mary and Joseph presented their infant son, *Yeshua*, in the Temple. He was their first–born, and according to Mosaic Law, each first–born male was to be presented to the priest at one month of age to be redeemed (Luke 2:22-38). The ceremony, called *Pidyon Haben* ("Redemption of the Son") redeemed the first–born son from full–time service through the payment of five shekels to the priest (Numbers 18:16). Mary and Joseph raised Jesus in a devout, God–fearing home. Luke notes that "every year his parents went to Jerusalem for the Feast of Passover" (Luke 2:41).

Throughout his earthly ministry Jesus taught that his mission was not to destroy the Law, but to fulfill it (Matthew 5:17). He often chose the national festivals as settings to make astonishing statements about himself, his Father, his relationship to the Word of God and to the world he came to save. In the Gospel of John alone, a surprising majority of the content is given to Jesus' ministry at the great feasts of Israel. Of the 879 verses in John's gospel, 660 (75%) directly relate to events occurring before, during or immediately following one of the feasts.

Jewish feasts are by definition religious services accompanied by demonstrations of joy and gladness. The noted exception is Yom Kippur, which is a day of fasting. The feasts commanded by God are most fully defined in Leviticus 23 where they are called "holy convocations." Except for those established after the Babylonian exile, such as Purim and Hanukkah, times for the feasts were fixed by divine appointment. During these holy convocations the people met before God to celebrate, to learn and to remember important spiritual and historic truths.

The seven original feasts described in Leviticus 23 have been characterized as God's calendar—a divine calendar celebrating the past, sanctifying the present and prophesying concerning the future. In this short chapter of only 44 verses, God instituted the annual sacred feasts of Israel. Although mentioned elsewhere in Scripture, the essential and primary requirements of the feasts are here gathered in their simplest form so that no one could ignore them. Thus, chapter 23 of Leviticus is one of the most fascinating and enlightening chapters in the Bible.

Before the destruction of the Temple by the Romans in 70 A.D., Jews had to comply with each meticulous detail recorded in the twenty-third chapter of Leviticus. There could be no error in commemorating the feasts. One mistake in the celebration of the Day of Atonement, for example, would result in banishment from the nation!

This divine calendar is not only sacred to the Jewish people; it is also the priceless heritage of every Christian, those who have "found the one Moses wrote about in the Law, and about whom the prophets also wrote—Jesus of Nazareth, the son of Joseph" (John 1:45).

It should come as no surprise that Gentiles are included in the blessing connected with the feasts. God's unconditional covenant with Abraham promised that "through (his) offspring all nations on earth will be blessed ..." (Genesis 22:18). As

Jesus instructed the Samaritan woman whom he met at Jacob's well in Sychar, "Salvation is from the Jews" (John 4:22).

Shabbat Shalom

Preceding the catalog of appointed feasts, God provides three verses of instruction for the most important day of the sacred calendar, *Shabbat*—the Sabbath (Leviticus 23:1-3). In keeping Shabbat one discovers the foundation and validity of all the feasts for "God blessed the seventh day and made it holy, because on it he rested from all the work of creating that he had done" (Genesis 2:3).

Far from a day of gloom and dismay, Shabbat is a time of happiness and encouragement. The Sabbath is God's precious gift to his people. It is a day in which the creature thankfully recognizes the majesty and goodness of his Creator. On this day he acknowledges his special relationship to God who is his peace—his *Shabbat Shalom* ("Sabbath peace").

Shabbat is a day of joy and hope even in the midst of sorrow and despair. Elie Wiesel, Holocaust survivor and acclaimed writer of our time, recalls how the memory of Shabbat engendered hope during dark days of despair in Auschwitz and Buchenwald. In these concentration camps he would reminisce of happy boyhood days when "with the advent of Shabbat, the town changed into a kingdom whose madmen and beggars became the princes of Shabbat." Wiesel continues with vivid memories that define the essence of Shabbat:

> *I shall never forget Shabbat in my town. When I shall have forgotten everything else, my memory will still retain the atmosphere of holiday, of serenity pervading even the poorest house: the white tablecloth, the candles, the meticulously combed little girls, the men on their way to synagogue. When*

my town shall fade into the abyss of time, I will continue to remember the light and the warmth it radiated on Shabbat. The exalting prayer, the wordless songs of the Hasidim (pious), the fire and radiance of their Masters.

  On that day of days, past and future suffering and anguish faded into the distance ... The jealousies and grudges, the petty rancors between neighbors could wait. As could the debts and worries, the dangers. Everything could wait. As it enveloped the universe, the Shabbat conferred on it a dimension of peace, an aura of love.[1]

Seven Feasts of the Lord

Celebrate the Feasts of the Lord will follow the festival chronology of Leviticus 23, with two post–exilic feasts reserved for the two concluding chapters. The appointed feasts of the Lord recorded in Leviticus 23 include:

1. The Passover—*Pesach* (verses 4-5)
2. The Feast of Unleavened Bread—(verses 6-8)
3. The Feast of Firstfruits—(verses 9-14)
4. The Feast of Pentecost—*Shavuot* (verses 15-21)
5. The Feast of Trumpets—*Rosh Hashanna* (verses 23-25)
6. The Day of Atonement—*Yom Kippur* (verses 26-32)
7. The Feast of Tabernacles—*Sukkot* (verses 33-43)

These seven feasts of Israel foresee and typify the progression, timing and implication of the major events of Jesus' redemptive ministry on earth. They commence at Calvary where the Lamb of God voluntarily gave himself for the sins of the world (*Pesach*—Passover), and culminate with the establishment of the messianic Kingdom at Jesus' second coming (*Sukkot*—

---

[1]Elie Wiesel, *A Jew Today* (New York: Random House, Inc., 1978), 9.

Jerusalem in Jesus' Day

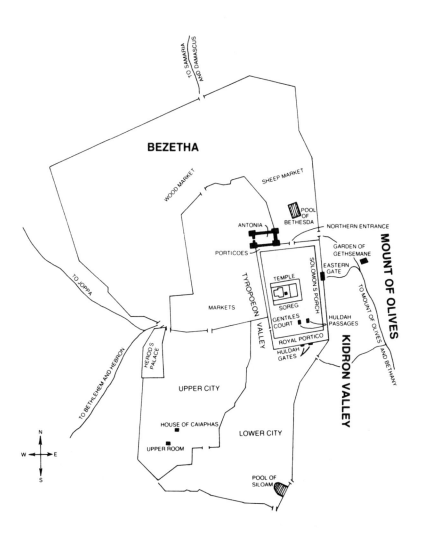

Tabernacles). We will discover that these are self–evident truths, without need to distort texts or misinterpret truth.

Messianic Prophecies

Each of the seven holy celebrations are mentioned throughout the Old and New Testaments. They have both symbolic and prophetic significance. The New Testament clearly teaches that some of the feasts have been fulfilled by the life and death of the Messiah, Jesus Christ. The prophetic implications of the fall festivals are yet to be fulfilled.

The following chart indicates the feasts that have been fulfilled and those that will be fulfilled (see also the full chart on page 128):[2]

Fulfilled	**To Be Fulfilled**
Leviticus 23:4-21	Leviticus 23:23-44
Passover	Trumpets
Unleavened Bread	Atonement
Firstfruits	Tabernacles
Pentecost	

Now, let us go up to Jerusalem for the feasts. "That is where the tribes go up, the tribes of the LORD, to praise the name of the LORD according to the statute given to Israel" (Psalm 122:4).

---

[2]Daniel Fuchs, *Israel's Holy Days*, (Neptune, N.J.: Loizeaux Brothers, 1985), 12.

...*To Ponder*

• Read: Deuteronomy 16:1-17

1. Why did God instruct the children of Israel to observe the Feasts of the Lord? (As you read the text, make a list of God's intentions in gathering his people at the great feasts.)

• Read: John 1:1-2:12

2. What unique attributes and characteristics of Jesus recorded in John 1 qualify him to be the long-awaited Messiah—the embodiment and fulfillment of the first four feasts?

3. John heralds Jesus as:

_____ (1:1)   _____ (1:29)

_____ (1:4)   _____ (1:41)

_____ (1:7)   _____ (1:49)

_____ (1:18)   _____ (1:51)

4. As Messiah, what was Jesus' relationship to the following:

    a. Eternity (1:1)

    b. God's creation (1:3)

    c. God's chosen people—the Jews (John 1:11)

    d. Believers (1:12)

    e. Mosaic Law (1:17)

    f. John the Baptist (1:23)

    g. His disciples (2:11)

5. How did Jesus' first miracle at Cana support and authenticate Old Testament prophecies and Jesus' own testimony?

Chapter 2

Pesach—Passover

This is a day you are to commemorate; for the generations to come you shall celebrate it as a festival to the LORD—a lasting ordinance ... Celebrate the Feast of Unleavened Bread, because it was on this very day that I brought your divisions out of Egypt. Celebrate this day as a lasting ordinance for the generations to come.

—Exodus 12:14, 17

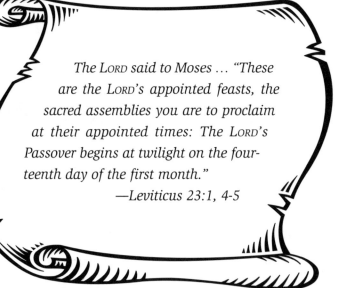

The Lᴏʀᴅ said to Moses … "These
are the Lᴏʀᴅ's appointed feasts, the
sacred assemblies you are to proclaim
at their appointed times: The Lᴏʀᴅ's
Passover begins at twilight on the fourteenth day of the first month."

—Leviticus 23:1, 4-5

*T*he Bible describes the Hebrew month of Nisan (March–April) as "the beginning of months." Although it no longer signals the official Jewish New Year, observed as Rosh Hashanna in the fall, it stands first because on the fourteenth of Nisan, Passover (Pesach), the most important of all the feasts, is celebrated.

During Nisan the ancient Israelites marched from slavery to freedom—from the land of Egypt toward the land God had promised them. The celebration of that renowned journey makes Nisan so sacred and celebratory that throughout this month eulogies are customarily not presented at funerals and public mourning is forbidden.

The name Nisan comes from Nissanu, the first month on the Babylonian calendar. The Bible does not use this name. It simply refers to the first month as the head of all other months. Each other month is numbered in its relationship to Nisan. Even the month of Tishri (see chapters 6, 7 and 8), distinctive as the beginning of the civil new year in Second Temple times, is still the seventh month on the Hebrew calendar—sixth after Nisan.

Nisan has another biblical name, *hodesh ha'aviv*, the month of spring. Symbols of spring surface throughout the Passover ritual.

Passover is unique among the religious festivals of the world. Celebrated for more than three millennia, Passover is the oldest continuously observed feast in existence today. It is the only feast that predates the giving of the Law to Moses on Mount Sinai. It was celebrated on the one year anniversary of the Exodus (Numbers 9:1-14); four days after the children of Israel came into the Promised Land (Joshua 4:19; 5:10-12); in the days of King Hezekiah (2 Chronicles 30) and King Josiah (2 Kings 23:21-

23); after the return from the Babylonian captivity (Ezra 6:19-
20); and in Jesus' day (John 11:55). Today, more Jewish people
celebrate Passover than any other Jewish holiday.

The Lord's Passover

Since Moses and the children of Israel had recently experienced the momentous events recorded in Exodus 12 and following chapters, God gives but a single verse of direction for
Passover in Leviticus: "The LORD's Passover begins at twilight
on the fourteenth day of the first month" (Leviticus 23:5). God's
earlier charge was fresh in their memory:

> *This is a day you are to commemorate; for the generations to
> come you shall celebrate it as a festival to the LORD—a lasting
> ordinance (Exodus 12:14).*

Thus, the People of the Covenant annually have celebrated
their deliverance from Egypt and the establishment of Israel as
a nation by God's redemptive act.

The Hebrew noun *Pesach* is derived from the verb *Pasach*,
the origin of which is unknown. Scholars have suggested a
variety of meanings, including "to pass over" (NIV, RSV), "to
skip by, spare" (1 Kings 18:21, 26, RSV) and "to defend, pro-
tect, stand guard over" (NEB). God promised the captive Hebrew people, "When I see the blood, I will pass over [spare,
protect] you" (Exodus 12:13).

God made certain that there were no excuses for missing
Passover. Since Jewish holidays are based on the lunar calendar rather than today's solar calendar, even those who could
not read or understand a calendar would notice the commencement of Passover. While one cannot discern the time of the
month by looking at the sun, the phases of the moon provide

a dependable, accurate timetable. Each lunar month starts with a new moon, reaching a full moon in the middle of the twenty–nine/thirty–day cycle. Thus, Passover always commenced when the first full moon of spring ascended in the heavens.

Passover was one of three festivals at which all males in Israel were obligated to "appear before the LORD." The biblical injunction of Deuteronomy 16:16-17 required mandatory attendance at the Feasts of Passover, Pentecost and Tabernacles. Included in the command were three specific requisites:

1. All males were to appear before the Lord.
2. They were not to attend the feast empty–handed.
3. Every man was to bring an offering in proportion to the blessing of God on his life.

In view of the Deuteronomic command, Jews everywhere had an intense desire to walk across the inner court of the Temple to pray, to hear the Levitical choir and to offer the Passover sacrifice.

The biblical record provides only three instructions for the observance of Passover. Special sacrifices were to be offered in the Temple each day of the feast (Leviticus 23:8; Numbers 28:19-24). Since the first and seventh days of the feast were days of sacred convocation, akin to Sabbaths, work was strictly prohibited on these days (Exodus 12:16; Leviticus 23:7-8; Numbers 28:25; Deuteronomy 16:8). Leaven (*hametz*, literally "sour") was strictly forbidden. Six passages stress the prohibition of using leaven during the feast (Exodus 12:14-20; 13:6-8; 23:15; 34:18; Leviticus 23:6; Deuteronomy 16:3,8).

Last Meal in Egypt

The description in Exodus 12:1-13:16 outlines the historical backdrop and ordinances regulating the last meal in Egypt

—the precursor of the Seder Meal:[1]

1. The celebration commenced at the full moon (Exodus 12:6) of "the first month" of spring. The month was originally called Abib. Following the Babylonian Captivity it was known as Nisan.

2. On the tenth of the month a year–old male lamb, without blemish, was chosen according to the size of the household (vv. 3-5).

3. At twilight on the 14th of the month the lamb was killed (v. 6).

4. The leaf of a hyssop plant was dipped in a basin filled with the slain lamb's blood. The blood was flung on the doorpost and lintels of the houses where the passover lamb was consumed (vv. 7, 22).

5. The lamb was roasted over the fire (head, legs and inner parts) making sure that no bones were broken (v. 8).

6. Matzah (bread made without yeast) and Merorim (bitter herbs) were eaten together with the meat of the sacrifice (v. 8).

7. The unconsumed parts of the meat were burned (v. 10).

8. The meal was eaten in haste with the robe tucked under the belt, sandals on the feet and staff in hand (v. 11).

9. Future generations were to celebrate Passover as a lasting ordinance.

10. All slaves and immigrants were permitted to join the Passover meal, as long as they were circumcised (vv. 44, 48).

[1] Marvin R. Wilson, Our Father Abraham, (Grand Rapids: William B. Eerdmans Publishing Company, 1989), 240.

Seder Meal

The Hebrew word *Seder* means "order," alluding to the prescribed order of the sacred ceremony. The Seder meal itself is quite lengthy. Throughout the observance, the Passover story is recounted through numerous prayers, songs, narrative readings and symbolic activities. The ritual usually lasts four to five hours. Special arrangements are made for seating. The leader sits at the head of the table. The youngest sits at his right side in order to fulfill a special role later in the service. The guest of honor is seated to the left of the leader, or sometimes this is the place reserved for the prophet Elijah.

The Seder has changed little since Jesus' day. This sacred meal of remembrance is divided into 15 orders with sub-sections. (The **bold print** indicates its reference in the gospel accounts of the Last Supper that will be discussed later.) The orders include:

1. *Birkat Haner*—Kindling of the Candles
    • It is the mother of the house who ushers in the holiday by lighting the Passover candles. She then covers her eyes with her hands and recites a blessing over the candles:
      "Blessed art Thou, O Lord our God, King of the Universe, Who has set us apart by his Word, and in whose Name we light the festival lights."

2. *Kiddush*—**First Cup: "The Cup of Blessing"**
    (Luke 22:14-18)
    • Following the blessing, the first of four cups of wine is consumed. (Grape juice is an acceptable substitute.) Since wine is often a biblical symbol of joy, four cups of wine are taken during the Seder to mirror the four-

fold joy for the Lord's redemption.[2] According to the Talmud (meaning "teachings," a collection of parables, sayings and commentary by Jewish sages concerning the Torah—five books of Moses), the four cups "were ordained to symbolize the four expressions of redemption (found in the "I Will" pronouncements in Exodus 6:6-7)" (*Talmud Yerushalmi—Pesachim 10*):

1. "I will bring you out"
2. "I will free you from being slaves"
3. "I will redeem you"
4. "I will take you as my own people"

3. *Urchatz*—Washing of the Hands
   • The hands are washed without the usual benediction.

4. *Karpas*—Dipping of the Parsley
   • Greens are dipped in salt water, reminiscent of the Red Sea and the tears of an enslaved people. The following blessing is recited:
   Blessed are you, O Lord our God, King of the Universe, Creator of the fruits of the earth.

5. *Yachatz*—Breaking of the Middle Matzah
   • The leader of the Seder takes the middle matzah from the three–sectioned special covering called a *matzah tash* (linen bag) and breaks it in two. He leaves one half in the middle section between the two whole matzahs and wraps the other half, called the *afikomen*, in a linen cloth. The afikomen is then "hidden" for the children to find later.

---

[2] Kevin Howard and Marvin Rosenthal, *The Feasts of the Lord*, (Orlando, Fla.: Zion's Hope, Inc., 1997), 55.

6. *Maggid*—The Story of the Passover
   • The story of the Exodus is retold from Exodus 12:1-13.
   • The matzahs are uncovered and the leader of the Seder lifts the matzah tash as everyone recites a blessing.
   • The matzah tash is returned to the table and the second cup of wine is poured.

a. *Ma–Nishtanah*—The Four Questions
   • The youngest member of the family stands and asks four questions, the defining theme of each being, "Why is this night different from all other nights?" The oldest member of the family solemnly replies to each prescribed question:

   1. "On all other nights we eat either leavened or unleavened bread; why on this night do we eat only matzah which is unleavened bread?"

   2. "On all other nights we eat vegetables and herbs of all kinds; why on this night do we eat only bitter herbs?"

   3. "On all other nights we never think of dipping herbs in water or in anything else; why on this night do we dip the parsley in salt water and the bitter herbs in charoseth?"

   4. "On all other nights we eat either sitting upright or reclining; why on this night do we all recline?"

   The leader of the Seder replies:

   "I am glad you asked these questions. This night is different from all other nights, because on this night we celebrate the going forth of the Jewish people from slavery into freedom.

   "Why do we eat only matzah tonight? When Pharaoh let our forefathers go from Egypt they were forced to flee in great haste. They had no time to bake their bread and could not wait for the yeast to rise. The sun which beat down on the dough as they carried it along baked it into unleavened bread called matzah.

"Why do we eat bitter herbs tonight? Because our forefathers were slaves in Egypt and their lives were made very bitter.

"Why do we dip the herbs twice tonight? We dip the parsley in salt water because it reminds us of the green of springtime. We dip the bitter herbs in sweet charoseth to remind us that our forefathers were able to withstand bitter slavery, because it was sweetened by the hope of freedom.

"Why do we recline at table? Because reclining was a sign of a free man long ago, and since our forefathers were freed on this night, we recline at the table."

b. *Makkot*—Second Cup: The Cup of Plagues

• As each of the ten plagues is read, a drop of wine is poured on a plate from the second cup. The leader says: "These are the ten plagues, which the Most Holy, blessed be He, brought on the Egyptians in Egypt:"

Dam	Blood
Ts'fardei'a	Frogs
Kinim	Vermin
Arov	Flies
Dever	Pestilence
Sh'chin	Boils
Barad	Hail
Arbe	Locusts
Choshech	Darkness
Makat Bechorot	Slaying the First–born

- Everyone joins in joyously singing *Dayenu* ("We would have been satisfied")
- First Half of the Hallel (Psalms of praise for Israel's redemption) is Recited (Psalms 113-114)

7. *Rachatz*—Washing of the Hands
   - The hands are washed with the usual benediction.

8. *Motzi–Matza*—Eating of the Unleavened Bread

9. *Maror*—Eating of the Bitter Herbs

10. *Korekh*—Eating of the Bitter Herbs with Charoseth

11. *Shulchan Orech*—**Passover Supper**
    (Matthew 26:22-26; Mark 14:17-20)

12. *Tzaphun*—**Eating of the Afikomen**
    (Matthew 26:26; Mark 14:22; Luke 22:19)
    - The children search for the *afikomen*. The leader redeems it by giving a gift to the child who found it. The *afikomen* is broken in olive size pieces and distributed to each guest. Tradition contends that *afikomen* means "dessert" since it is the final food of the Seder feast. Some scholars believe that it comes from a root word meaning "I have come" (see Psalm 40:6-8), while others believe that it means "hidden."

13. *Birkat Hamazon*—The blessing after the meal

Ha–Geulah—Third Cup: The Cup of Redemption
    (Matthew 26:27; Mark 14:24; Luke 22:20)
    - The third cup is poured and elevated. The leader of the Seder leads the blessing: *"Ba–ruch Attah Ah–doh-nai Elo–hei–nu Me–lech Ha–olam Boh–ray Pree Ha-guw–fen."* (Blessed are you, O Lord our God, King of

the Universe, Creator of the fruit of the vine.)
- All drink the third cup of wine (preferably while reclining).
- Elijah's cup is filled with wine and the door is opened (usually by the youngest child) to see if Elijah has come. The door is then closed.

14. *Hallel*—Fourth Cup: The Cup of Praise
- Second Half of the Hallel is recited (Psalms 115-118)

15. *Nirtzah*—**Closing Hymn**
(Matthew 26:30; Mark 14:26)

Jesus' Last Seder

For the Christian, the Passover celebration recalls the sacrificial, atoning death of Christ, our Paschal Lamb. By understanding the ritual and symbolism of this celebration, Christians can more fully understand the apostle Paul's affirmation: "For Christ, our Passover Lamb, has been sacrificed..." (1 Corinthians 5:7).

Joyous pilgrims from all over the world thronged Jerusalem for Passover, *the* holy day—the Feast of Redemption. Jerusalem's streets were transformed into an animated collage of ethnic sights, sounds and smells. As it is today, the Passover was a festive time of sacrifice, sacred commemoration and a gala meal. By Jesus' time this distinctive meal was popularly known as the Seder.

On that ominous fourteenth of Nisan in first–century Jerusalem, Jesus celebrated the already ancient Passover meal with his disciples. It was to be his final Seder, and indeed his Last Supper, with his followers.

The gospel accounts of Jesus' final Seder with his disciples mention only two of the four seder cups—the first and third. According to Jewish custom, these two were the most important. The first cup sanctified the entire Passover ritual. However, the Mishnah (second century codification of the Oral Law) asserts that the third cup was the most important of all four. The third cup was the "Cup of Redemption."

At the conclusion of the meal, everyone washed his hands for the third time. Jesus then poured the third cup, the Cup of Redemption (see 1 Corinthians 10:16). He broke the bread, known today as the afikomen, and recited the prayer of thanksgiving, the *Birkat Hamazon.* As Matthew recounts the scene, "Jesus took bread, gave thanks and broke it, and gave it to his disciples, saying, 'Take and eat; this is my body'" (Matthew 26:26).

Jesus elevated the third cup he had recently poured and offered it to his disciples with the mystical admonition, "Drink from it, all of you. This is my blood of the new covenant, which is poured out for many for the forgiveness of sins" (Matthew 26:27-28). Each disciple sipped and passed the common cup, following which they recited Psalms 115-118, the second part of the Hallel (see *Hallel*, #14 above).

Jesus then surprised his disciples. He refused to drink the fourth cup of wine—the "Cup of Praise." Jesus explained, "I tell you, I will not drink of this fruit of the vine from now on until that day when I drink it anew with you in my Father's kingdom" (Matthew 26:29). He knew that the time of his acceptance was in the future, and his joy would not be full until then.

The celebrated Passover meal concluded with the traditional singing of a hymn—"When they had sung a hymn, they went out to the Mount of Olives" (Matthew 26:30).

Mysteries of the Atonement

For the believer, Passover both illustrates and embodies our salvation. It is more than a feast commemorating the exodus from Egypt. It transcends the varying theologies and liturgical forms of the sacrament. Fundamentally, the Passover instructs the believer in the mysteries of the Atonement (Ephesians 3:4-6) and in living a sacramental life (Ephesians 1:9; 5:32).

The Salvation Army's renowned poet–General, Albert Orsborn, captured the quintessence of the Passover Seder celebrated by the Lord and his disciples. As Christ's twentieth century disciples, let us affirm:

> *My life must be Christ's broken bread,*
> *My love his outpoured wine,*
> *A cup o'erfilled, a table spread*
> *Beneath his name and sign,*
> *That other souls, refreshed and fed,*
> *May share his life through mine.*[3]

---

[3] *The Song Book of The Salvation Army* (Verona, NJ: The Salvation Army, 1987), no. 512, p. 142.

... *To Ponder*

• Read: Deuteronomy 16:16-17

1. Why do you think God required attendance at the three feasts of obligation listed in Deuteronomy 16:16-17?

• Read: Psalm 125:1-2; 128:5-6; 130:6-8; and 134

2. Since Jerusalem sits on Israel's central ridge at 2,427 feet above sea level, people traveling from any direction must "*go up* to Jerusalem." Along the way (and especially when the Eternal City came into view) pilgrims would joyously sing the Songs of Ascents (Psalms 120 through 134) to the accompaniment of flutes. Make a list of the timeless promises found in the above referenced passages from Psalm 125, 128, 130 and 134.

• Read: John 2:23-3:21

This is the second record of Jesus going "up to Jerusalem" (2:13) to celebrate Passover. His first recorded attendance at Passover was with his family when he was 12 years old (Luke 2:41-52).

3. Why do you think that Nicodemus, a Pharisee, came to Jesus under the cover of darkness during Passover? What were his fears? What was his fundamental question?

4. Jesus' reply to Nichodemus' question was startling and direct: "No one can see the kingdom of God unless he is born again" (3:3). Reflect on the correlation of "new birth" with the Passover celebration, i.e., the "beginning of months"; Israel's experience of national rebirth upon leaving Egypt; the sound of the taskmaster's whip replaced by the song of deliverance; the Passover Lamb; the blood and escape from judgment, and the jubilant procession through the bridled waters of the Red Sea.

Chapter 3

Hag Hamatozt—
Unleavened Bread

It's only ordinary
unleavened bread
Ordinary matzah
On an earthen plate
It probably came
From a supermarket shelf
A Manischewitz box
Ordinary matzoh
Blessed for Passover
Oh, but when I take it
And cradle it lovingly
In my hands
Break it and bless it
It is for me
Most Holy Bread
Good Friday Bread

Body of the Lamb that was slain
With my cup of Redemption
Communion Bread
Lechem without hametz
Without yeast of sin
Pierced
Striped
Bruised
Shrouded afikomen
Hidden
Then resurrected
With glory
I partake
Alleluia, alleluia
Alleluia, alleluia, alleluia!
                    —Maude Carolan

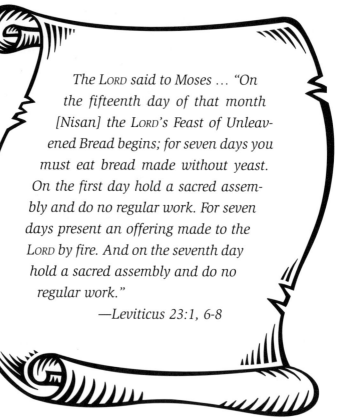

The LORD said to Moses ... "On the fifteenth day of that month [Nisan] the LORD's Feast of Unleavened Bread begins; for seven days you must eat bread made without yeast. On the first day hold a sacred assembly and do no regular work. For seven days present an offering made to the LORD by fire. And on the seventh day hold a sacred assembly and do no regular work."

—Leviticus 23:1, 6-8

*I*srael's ancient calendar commenced with Passover and the Feast of Unleavened Bread. Originally, these were separate feasts. According to Leviticus 23, Passover was celebrated at twilight on the fourteenth of Nisan (Exodus 12:6). The Feast of Unleavened Bread commenced on the fifteenth of Nisan, lasting seven days until the twenty–first day of the month (Exodus 12:15, 18; Leviticus 23:5-6; Numbers 28:16-17; 2 Chronicles 35:1, 17).

The Old Testament distinguishes the festivals (Exodus 34:18, 25) by using the expressions "Passover Feast" (*hag ha–pesach*) and "Feast of Unleavened Bread" (*hag ha–matzot*). *Matzah* and the plural *matzot* are the Hebrew words for "unleavened bread."

Miraculous Emancipation

The Feast of Unleavened Bread is a reminder of Israel's miraculous emancipation from Egyptian bondage. Since the children of Israel fled in haste, there was no time for the bread dough to rise (Exodus 12:39). Therefore, God commanded:

> *For seven days eat unleavened bread, the bread of affliction, because you left Egypt in haste—so that all the days of your life you may remember the time of your departure from Egypt (Deuteronomy 16:3).*

Since the celebrations of Passover and Unleavened Bread were so close together, they were customarily treated as one feast in both the Old and New Testaments (see Matthew 26:17, Mark 14:1, Luke 22:1). Although the title "Feast of Unleavened Bread" was still used in Jesus' day, the first century historian Josephus indicates that "Passover" was commonly used to refer to both festivals (Josephus, *Antiquities of the Jews* 14.2.1; 17.9.3.)

Bread Without Yeast

God commanded the children of Israel to eat only pure unleavened bread (made without yeast) during the week following Passover:

> *Eat unleavened bread during those seven days; nothing with yeast in it is to be seen among you, nor shall any yeast be seen anywhere within your borders (Exodus 13:7).*

Not only was the consumption of leaven forbidden during the feast, but even the presence of leaven in one's house was prohibited. Yeast was not "to be seen" during this sacred week. The consequences of not obeying this command were severe. God required the children of Israel to "remove the yeast from your houses, for whoever eats anything with yeast in it from the first day through the seventh must be cut off from Israel" (Exodus 12:15). Deuteronomy 16:4 emphasizes the magnitude of the regulation: "Let no yeasts be found in your possession *in all your land* (emphasis mine) for seven days."

As previously noted, the Hebrew word for leaven is *hametz,* which literally means "sour." Leaven (yeast or baking powder) produces fermentation. As the leaven "sours" the bread dough, small gas bubbles make the dough rise. Leaven is an agent of dynamic growth.

With few exceptions in Scripture, leaven represented evil or error. Leaven is the agent that causes fermentation. Jesus used the same metaphor when he warned his disciples to "be careful … be on your guard against the yeast of the Pharisees and Sadducees" (Matthew 16:6, 11; Mark 8:15).

Abstaining from leaven for seven days symbolized the desire to be a holy people and experience a holy walk with the Lord. Passover underscored redemption from bondage through the Paschal sacrifice. The Feast of Unleavened Bread reminded the celebrants that, because of their redemption, they must live a life cleansed from sin.

The Bread of Life

The apostle Paul precisely applies the dual metaphors of the Paschal lamb and unleavened bread to characterize Christ's sacrificial death:

> *Get rid of the old yeast that you may be a new batch without yeast—as you really are. For Christ, our Passover lamb, has been sacrificed. Therefore let us keep the Festival, not with the old yeast, the yeast of malice and wickedness, but with bread without yeast, the bread of sincerity and truth (1 Corinthians 5:7, 8).*

The unleavened bread of the New Covenant is the body of Christ. Jesus made this clear during the Last Supper. Toward the end of the meal, he took the unleavened bread, broke it and gave it to his disciples saying, "This is my body given for you…" (Luke 22:19).

It is significant, and hardly coincidental, that Jesus was born in *Bet–Lehem* ("house of bread"). Think of it! On a quiet night two thousand years ago, an event took place in this hamlet that forever changed the course of history. The child born in a bleak, barren Bethlehem stable would one day declare in the Capernaum synagogue, "I am the bread of life … I am the living bread that came down from heaven…" (John 6:35, 51).

Jesus' claim is not a clever, self–serving metaphor. The glorious truth is that as God sustained the children of Israel in the wilderness, his Son now feeds the believer on the Bread of Life. Jesus declared:

Herodian Palestine During Christ's Ministry

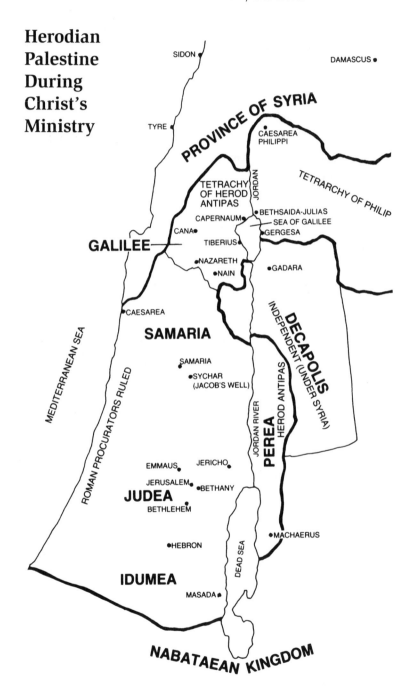

SIDON

DAMASCUS ●

PROVINCE OF SYRIA

TYRE ●

CAESAREA PHILIPPI ●

TETRARCHY OF PHILIP

TETRACHY OF HEROD ANTIPAS

JORDAN

CAPERNAUM ●

● BETHSAIDA-JULIAS

SEA OF GALILEE

CANA ●

GERGESA

GALILEE

TIBERIUS ●

● NAZARETH

● NAIN

● GADARA

MEDITERRANEAN SEA

● CAESAREA

SAMARIA

DECAPOLIS

INDEPENDENT (UNDER SYRIA)

SAMARIA ●

● SYCHAR (JACOB'S WELL)

ROMAN PROCURATORS RULED

JORDAN RIVER

HEROD ANTIPAS

PEREA

EMMAUS ●

JERICHO ●

JERUSALEM ●

● BETHANY

JUDEA

BETHLEHEM

● HEBRON

● MACHAERUS

DEAD SEA

IDUMEA

MASADA ●

NABATAEAN KINGDOM

It is not Moses who has given you the bread from heaven,
but it is my Father who gives you the true bread from heaven.
For the bread of God is he who comes down from heaven and
gives life to the world (John 6:32-33).

The bread used by Jews in celebrating Passover is called
matzah ("unleavened"). Most commercially produced matzah
today is striped, and it is pierced. It is a contemporary, visible
reminder that the Messiah, although pure and sinless, carried
the stripes of the Roman whip. The soldiers pierced his hands
and feet with nails, and his side with a spear. Isaiah proph-
esied of this momentous event seven centuries earlier:

Surely he took up our infirmities and carried our sorrows,
yet we considered him stricken by God, smitten by him, and
afflicted. But he was pierced for our transgressions, he was
crushed for our iniquities; the punishment that brought us
peace was upon him, and by his wounds we are healed (Isaiah
53:4-5).

May our daily communion with Christ be marked by a
conspicuous, persistent, holy, unleavened walk. It is a marvelous possibility because "God made him who had no sin to be
sin for us, so that in him we might become the righteousness
of God" (2 Corinthians 5:21). Hallelujah!

...*To Ponder*

• Read: John 6:1-59

1. "The Jewish Passover Feast was near" (6:4), and Jesus was preparing to do the impossible. With a boy's lunch, he was about to feed five thousand men, besides the women and children. The gospel writers offer rational reasons why it could not be done. What were the negatives?

    a. Luke 9:12 _____

    b. Luke 9:13 _____

    c. John 6:7 _____

    d. Matthew 14:15a _____

    e. Matthew 14:15b _____

2. The day following the miracle, Jesus taught in the synagogue in Capernaum using bread as a metaphor for spiritual sustenance. Reflect on the progression of Jesus' instruction:

    a. "You are looking for me ... because you ate the loaves and had your fill" (6:26).

    b. "It is not Moses who has given you the bread from heaven, but my Father who gives you the true bread from heaven. For the bread of God is he who comes down from heaven and gives life to the world" (6:32-33).

    c. "I am the bread of life. He who comes to me will never go hungry..." (6:35).

d. "I am the living bread that came down from heaven. If anyone eats of this bread, he will live forever. This bread is my flesh, which I will give for the life of the world" (6:51).

e. "This is the bread that came down from heaven. Your forefathers ate manna and died, but he who feeds on this bread will live forever" (6:58).

3. Reflect on the fundamental connection between the *written* word and the *living* Word. Compare the seasonal selections in the following Old Testament passages and the pronouncements of Jesus recorded in the sixth chapter of John:

   a. Isaiah 55:2   and   John 6:27

   b. Isaiah 54:13   and   John 6:45

   c. Numbers 11:13   and   John 6:51, 55

   d. Genesis 3:3   and   John 6:50

   e. Genesis 3:22   and   John 6:51

   f. Genesis 3:24   and   John 6:37

Chapter 4

Firstfruits

Along life's way there walks
 with us
 A Man whom we know not.
Our eyes are holden, and
 our minds
 With fear are overwrought.
Yet as He speaks our hearts
 awake—
 This Stranger knows us well!
Can He be here whom death
 had claimed?
 Is Jesus with us still?

He takes the age–old prophecies
 In mist enshrouded long,
And lo! the ancient word is clear,
 The book breaks into song.

Its every line aglow with grace
 As sacred pages turn.
Should not our souls leap
 up in joy,
 Our hearts within us burn?

He passes down our street
 today.
 The street of common men,
He pauses at our board
 once more,
 He breaks the bread again.
And is not this Emmaus road
 He walks with us to Heaven?
Yes, every day is Easter day
 Now that the Lord is risen.
 —Edward Read

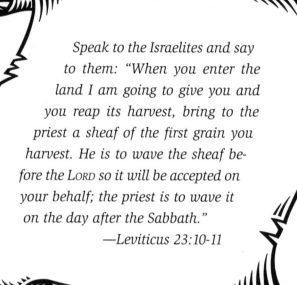

Speak to the Israelites and say to them: "When you enter the land I am going to give you and you reap its harvest, bring to the priest a sheaf of the first grain you harvest. He is to wave the sheaf before the Lᴏʀᴅ so it will be accepted on your behalf; the priest is to wave it on the day after the Sabbath."

—Leviticus 23:10-11

*P*assover week originally contained three main events: (1) the Paschal lamb was slain on the fourteenth of Nisan, (2) the Feast of Unleavened Bread commenced on the fifteenth of Nisan, and (3) the Feast of Firstfruits followed "on the day after the Sabbath," the sixteenth of Nisan.

Christians call this feast *Easter*, after the Babylonian deity, Ishtar, the goddess of fertility. While the contemporary celebration incorporates objects of fertility—rabbits, eggs and new clothes—the original Hebrew feast commemorated God's replenishing of the earth each spring.

Firstfruits Controversy

The Feast of Firstfruits is an enigma today. It essentially has not been observed since the destruction of the Temple in 70 A.D. Jews today do not consider Firstfruits to coincide with the Feast of Unleavened Bread. Instead, they apply the term Firstfruits to Shavuot (Pentecost). For Jews today, the feast described in this chapter is not a feast at all. The event is referred to as *Sefirat Ha–Omer* ("the Counting of the Omer"), an offering that takes place on the second day of Unleavened Bread and commences the forty–nine day countdown culminating at Pentecost on the fiftieth day.

Although not regarded as a feast by Jews today, Christian scholars consider the "lasting ordinance" described in Leviticus 23:9-14 as a distinct feast. The Feast of Firstfruits incorporates timeless truths and contains a powerful message for God's people today.

Originally, Firstfruits was an early spring festival, the third of the seven feasts recorded in Leviticus 23. It took place on the sixteenth day of Nisan, the first month of the Hebrew calendar (March–April), two days following the beginning of Pesach (Passover). The Bible does not specify the calendar date of Firstfruits, but assigns its observance "on the day after the Sabbath" (Leviticus 23:11). Since the precise date was not given, many interpretations and much controversy followed.

The Sadducees believed that the Sabbath referred to the first Shabbat (Saturday) that occurred during Passover week. However, since Shabbat can refer to any holy day on which work is prohibited, the Pharisees (along with most of the Jews) believed that the Shabbat in question was the fifteenth of Nisan, the first day of the Feast of Unleavened Bread. That was a Shabbat—a day when they could do no work (Leviticus 23:7). The first-century Jewish historian Josephus, agreed with the Pharisees' interpretation. He wrote:

> But on the second day of unleavened bread, which is the sixteenth day of the month, they first partake of the fruits of the earth, for before that day they do not touch them (Josephus, Antiquities of the Jews 3.10.5).

The time line for the Passover season thus consists of three main events: Passover (14 Nisan), the Feast of Unleavened Bread (15-21 Nisan), and the Feast of Firstfruits (16 Nisan). Therefore, the second day of Unleavened Bread (16 Nisan) was also Firstfruits—two holidays on the same day.

The chronology is significant. As we will see later, according to the Pharisees and Josephus, Firstfruits fell on Sunday during the Passover events that included Jesus' death, burial and resurrection. Jesus rose from the dead on the Feast of Firstfruits!

Preparation, Procession and Presentation

On this joyous day, the early crops of the spring planting, the *first fruits*, were presented in the Temple. The Feast of

Firstfruits was not merely a harvest festival, however. It was an acknowledgment of Israel's total dependence on God. In gratitude and recognition of God's providential care, the people presented part of the fruit that ripened first.

The order of service for presentation of the firstfruits during the Temple days is fascinating and enlightening. The priests and members of the Sanhedrin solemnly marked the spot where the first barley sheaf was to be harvested during a formal ceremony on the fourteenth of Nisan. While there was no restriction on where the sheaf was to be cut, it must have grown in an ordinary field, without the aid of fertilizer or irrigation. Likely, the field was in or near the Kidron Valley, due east and within walking distance of the Temple.

Just after the sun went down on the fifteenth of Nisan (i.e., at the start of the sixteenth), three priests, each carrying a sickle and basket, set out to harvest the first barley sheaf. As they passed the large crowds that had gathered, they asked prescribed questions three times:

- "Has the sun gone down?"
- "With this sickle?"
- "Into this basket?"
- "Shall I reap?"

To each question, the crowd replied with a resounding *"Ken!"* (Yes). Reaching the appointed site, the trio cautiously cut the barley sheaf to the exact predetermined portion (*Menahot* 10:3).

The harvesters carefully transported the barley ears into the Temple court. They then beat the stalks with canes, so as not to injure the grain. Following further meticulous preparation, the priests received a small amount of flour (about five pints) to offer in the Temple that morning, the Feast of Firstfruits. Through this ceremony of consecration, the children of Israel joyously declared that they were not only offering the firstfruits to the Lord, but that the entire harvest belonged to him.

Christ—the Firstfruits

The New Testament tells of another harvest:

> But Christ has indeed been raised from the dead, the firstfruits of those who have fallen asleep. For since death came through a man, the resurrection of the dead comes also through a man. For as in Adam all die, so in Christ all will be made alive. But each in his own turn: Christ, the firstfruits; then, when he comes, those who belong to him (1 Corinthians 15:20-23; see also Revelation 1:5).

For the Christian, the Feast of Firstfruits pictures the resurrection of Christ and points forward to the time of climactic resurrection.

The chronology of the events leading up to the Resurrection is clear. Keeping in mind that the Hebrew day began at sunset and lasted until the following sunset (encompassing portions of two Roman days), we can construct the following sequence of events:

1. Jesus celebrated Passover with his disciples **Thursday** evening (14 Nisan);
2. He was hastily buried **Friday** afternoon (still 14 Nisan) before the onset of the Sabbath. As Mark records, "It was Preparation Day (that is, the day before the Sabbath). So as evening approached, Joseph of Arimathea, a prominent member of the Council, who was himself waiting for the Kingdom of God, went boldly to Pilate and asked for Jesus' body" (Mark 15:42-43; see also Luke 23:54 and John 19:42).

3. Jesus was dead in the tomb on the Sabbath, **Saturday**, the Feast of Unleavened Bread (15 Nisan). Matthew 27:62 indicates that it was "the next day, the one after Preparation Day," that the chief priests and the Pharisees went to Pilate to request that Jesus' body be guarded.

4. Jesus rose from the dead on **Sunday**, the Feast of Firstfruits (16 Nisan). Matthew notes that it was "after the Sabbath, at dawn on the first day of the week" that Mary Magdalene and her companion, Mary, went to the tomb (Matthew 28:1; see also Mark 16:1, Luke 24:1 and John 20:1).

All the gospel writers are careful to note the chronology of the events that perfectly parallel the three feasts of Passover, Unleavened Bread and Firstfruits.

Considering these obvious parallels, Christians miss a significant biblical truth by using the term Easter instead of Firstfruits. As the title implies, because there is a "first," there will follow a second, third, fourth and so on. In this sense, we do not only commemorate the resurrection of Jesus on the Feast of Firstfruits, but also celebrate the resurrection of all believers! The apostle Paul explicitly declares that Jesus Christ is Number *One*—the Firstfruit—and every believer, "those who belong to him" will follow "each in his own turn" (1 Corinthians 15:20-23). This is *Good News*, for not only did Christ rise from the dead, so will his followers one glorious day! Paul graphically depicts the scene:

> *For the Lord himself will come down from heaven, with a loud command, with the voice of the archangel and with the trumpet call of God, and the dead in Christ will rise first. After that, we who are still alive and are left will be caught*

up together with them in the clouds to meet the Lord in the air. And so we will be with the Lord forever (1 Thessalonians 4:16-17).

The Expectation

The Jews of Jesus' day had an understanding of resurrection. One of the most interesting expectations of resurrection is found in the apocalyptic book of Enoch, written during the first two centuries before Christ. The text speaks of a resurrection of the righteous, for the wicked "shall have no hope of rising from their beds, because they do not extol the name of the Lord of Spirits" (Enoch 46:6). The righteous, however, will be raised from their graves:

> And in those days shall the earth also give back that
>   which has been entrusted to it,
> And Sheol also shall give back that which it has received,
> And hell shall give back that which it owes.
> For in those days the Elect One (the Messiah) shall arise,
> And he shall choose the righteous and holy from among
>   them (the dead);
> For the day has drawn nigh that they should be saved
> (Enoch 51:1-2).

The Main Event

The resurrection of Christ from the dead is *the* event of history. All others pale in significance. The apostle Paul concludes, "If Christ has not been raised, our preaching is useless and so is your faith" (1 Corinthians 15:14).

The fact of the Resurrection dramatically transformed the disciples themselves. Philip Yancey observes, "One need only read the Gospels' descriptions of disciples huddling behind locked doors and then proceed to the descriptions in Acts of the same men proclaiming Christ openly in the streets and in jail cells to perceive the seismic significance of what took place on Easter Sunday. The Resurrection is the epicenter of belief."[1]

Yancey goes on to quote the acclaimed novelist John Updike who more poetically expresses the same poignant truth:

> *Make no mistake: if He rose at all*
> *it was as His body;*
> *if the cells' dissolution did not reverse, the molecules*
> *reknit, the amino acids rekindle,*
> *the Church will fall.*[2]

Festivals of Salvation

The three spring feasts reflect and parallel the spiritual chronology of the Christian walk. Our salvation is assured through the shed **blood** of Christ (Passover). Consequently, we walk in communion with him in a regenerated **body** (Unleavened Bread); someday we will be **resurrected** to walk with the Lord forever (Firstfruits).

Let us celebrate, as did Jesus, the radiant reality of all three festivals. Jesus observed his final Passover by eating the Seder with his disciples. His body was broken for us as he consecrated the Feast of Unleavened Bread in a borrowed tomb. He celebrated the Feast of Firstfruits by rising from the dead!

And so every Easter, every Feast of Firstfruits, we confidently proclaim, "The Lord is risen—He is risen indeed!"

---

[1] Philip Yancey, *The Jesus I Never Knew*, (Grand Rapids: Zondervan Publishing House, 1995), 217.

[2] John Updike, "Seven Stanzas at Easter," in *Collected Poems 1953-1993*, (New York: Alfred A. Knopf, 1993), 163.

... *To Ponder*

Although not as emphasized in the Hebrew Scriptures as other feasts, the Feast of Firstfruits forms a significant backdrop to New Testament teaching. Reflect on the following references in terms of what you have learned about the Feast of Firstfruits.

"Firstfruits" concerning:

1. *Individuals*—Epaenetus and the house of Stephanas were firstfruits of the gospel.

> "Salute my wellbeloved Epaenetus who is the first-fruits of Achaia unto Christ" (Romans 16:5, KJV).

> "The house of Stephanas ... (is) the firstfruits of Achaia..." (1 Corinthians 16:15, KJV).

2. *Israel*—God chose and blessed the patriarchs (the firstfruits) and therefore all of Israel (the whole batch).

> "If the part of the dough offered as firstfruits is holy, then the whole batch is holy; if the root is holy, so are the branches" (Romans 11:16).

> Accordingly, "God did not reject his people..." (Romans 11:2).

3. *Believers*—Believers are *set apart* to the Lord as his firstfruits.

> "He chose to give us birth through the word of truth, that we might be a kind of firstfruits of all he created" (James 1:18).

4. *Salvation*—The indwelling Spirit of God is the guarantee of our final redemption.

> "We ourselves, who have the firstfruits of the Spirit, groan inwardly as we wait eagerly for our adoption as sons, the redemption of our bodies" (Romans 8:23).

5. *The Rapture*—The 144,000 mentioned in Revelation 14 will serve as the guarantee or pledge (the firstfruits) of a future harvest within the nation of Israel. The result is summarized by the Apostle Paul: "And so all Israel will be saved..." (Romans 11:26).

> "These are those who did not defile themselves with women, for they kept themselves pure. They follow the Lamb wherever he goes. They were purchased from among men and offered as firstfruits to God and the Lamb" (Revelation 14:5).

Chapter 5

Shavuot—Pentecost

Thou Christ of burning, cleansing flame,
  Send the fire!
Thy blood–bought gift today we claim,
  Send the fire!
Look down and see this waiting host,
Give us the promised Holy Ghost,
We want another Pentecost,
  Send the fire!
                    —William Booth

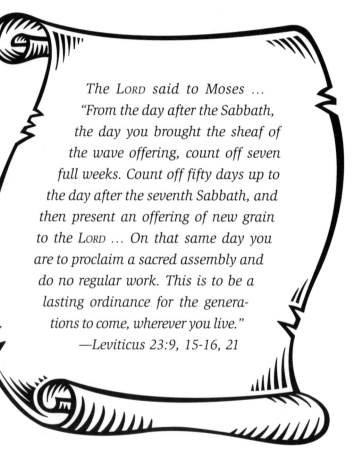

The LORD said to Moses ...
"From the day after the Sabbath,
the day you brought the sheaf of
the wave offering, count off seven
full weeks. Count off fifty days up to
the day after the seventh Sabbath, and
then present an offering of new grain
to the LORD ... On that same day you
are to proclaim a sacred assembly and
do no regular work. This is to be a
lasting ordinance for the generations to come, wherever you live."
—Leviticus 23:9, 15-16, 21

*P*entecost was the second of the three great festivals at which every male Israelite was obligated to "appear before the LORD." The biblical injunction of Deuteronomy 16:16-17 required attendance at the feasts of Passover, Pentecost and Tabernacles.

Seven Weeks Later

On the sixth day of Sivan (May–June), seven weeks and a day after offering the first harvested barley or the Feast of Firstfruits, the children of Israel celebrated the Feast of Weeks. As its name implies, the feast commenced seven weeks after Firstfruits—the fiftieth day after the waving of the sheaf of the first ripe barley (Leviticus 23:10). Biblically, this feast was never tied to a specific calendar date. It was instead defined as a calculation of fifty days—the day after seven weeks had passed from the Feast of Firstfruits. The feast's Greek name is *Pentecost*, or "fiftieth day" (Acts 2:1; 2 Maccabees 12:32). In Hebrew, the festival is known as *Shavuot*, meaning "weeks."

Summer Harvest and Giving of the Law

The Feast of Pentecost marked the summer harvest, the second of the year. It concluded the growing season that had ceremoniously commenced seven weeks earlier on the Feast of Firstfruits. In the year that Jesus died, both feasts, Firstfruits and Pentecost, were celebrated on a Sunday.

While Pentecost was initially a joyful celebration of Israel's grain harvest, the festival also commemorated the giving of the Law to Moses on Mount Sinai. Based on the biblical account of the arrival at Mount Sinai, Jewish tradition maintains that Moses received the Law exactly fifty days after the first Passover. The Bible records that it was "in the third month after the Israelites left Egypt—on the very day—they came to the Desert of Sinai" (Exodus 19:1). By the time of Christ, Pentecost was considered a dual festival marking the commencement of the summer harvest and the anniversary of the giving of the Law on Mount Sinai.

Offerings and Sacrifices

Leviticus 23:15-22 records numerous directions for observing the Feast of Pentecost. The day was to be considered a Sabbath. Ordinary labor was suspended, and a holy convocation proclaimed. The day commenced with the offering of two loaves of *leavened* bread, such as was daily used in a household. Following the customary morning sacrifice, the priests offered a burnt offering of "seven male lambs, each a year old and without a defect, one young bull and two rams" (Leviticus 23:18). Next, the priests presented a meal offering, a drink offering and a sin offering. The offerings culminated with a peace (or "fellowship") offering of "two lambs, each a year old" (Leviticus 23:19).

Note that the sin offering preceded the peace offering. The peace offering was not a mere entreaty for peace. It was a fervent expression of gratitude for the peace that results from God's acceptance of the sin offering. The two lambs offered as a peace offering during Pentecost marked the only public peace offering of the sacrificial year. This unique offering celebrated the peace and fellowship existing between God and those whom he has cleansed from sin.

God's final instruction for this festival focused on the needy:

> *When you reap the harvest of your land, do not reap to the very edges of your field or gather the gleanings of your harvest. Leave them for the poor and the alien. I am the* Lord *your God (Leviticus 23:22; see also Deuteronomy 16:10-12).*

The Mishnah (second century codification of the Oral Law) offers a vivid description of the Day of Pentecost before the destruction of the Temple by the Romans in 70 A.D.:

> *How were the first-fruits brought up? The populace that lives in the vicinity of the Assembly Head ... gathers together in his home town, and everyone sleeps the night in the town's streets. They do not enter into the houses (to circumvent becoming exposed to ritual impurity). Waking them in the morning, the overseer would cry out, "Get up, and let us go up to Zion, to the House of the Lord our God!"*
>
> *Those who were closest in the procession (to Jerusalem) would carry fresh dates and grapes ... Those at the back would carry dried fruits and raisins. An ox is led before them (designated as the offering to accompany the first-fruits) whose horns are overlaid with gold, with an olive branch crown on its head ...*
>
> *A flute was played at the head of the procession, whose sound could be heard from a great distance. Finally they reached the Temple Mount. Upon arriving at the Temple, (the procession) entered inside. Once in the outer court, the Levites would sing: "I will praise You, God, for You have lifted me up, and have not allowed my enemies to rejoice over me"* (Psalm 30:1)   —Tractate Bikurim 3.

Jerusalem's International Festival

Passover falls in late March to mid–April, and Pentecost comes 50 days later in late May or early June. Ideal traveling conditions made it possible for multitudes to make the pilgrimage to Jerusalem. As many people attended the Feast of Pentecost as Passover. This accounts for the extraordinary list of countries represented at the Feast of Pentecost recorded in the second chapter of Acts. Pentecost was *the* international day in Jerusalem

The Father's Gift

For Christians, the most celebrated Pentecost in history was the one following the resurrection and ascension of Christ. Before his ascension, Jesus commanded his disciples to tarry in Jerusalem. He provided explicit instructions:

> Do not leave Jerusalem, but wait for the gift my Father promised, which you have heard me speak about. For John baptized with water, but in a few days you will be baptized with the Holy Spirit (Acts 1:4).

Their wait was not long—about ten days following Christ's ascension. And then it happened. The Holy Spirit descended on 120 believers gathered in an upper room on Mount Zion. Luke concisely sets the scene:

> When the day of Pentecost came, they were all together in one place. Suddenly a sound like the blowing of a violent wind came from heaven and filled the whole house where they were sitting. They saw what seemed to be tongues of fire that separated and came to rest on each of them. All of them were filled with the Holy Spirit ... (Acts 2:1-3a).

During this extraordinary Pentecost, the Holy Spirit descended and breathed transforming life into the followers of Jesus. At that sudden, distinct, divine moment, the church was born!

The fledgling church experienced staggering growth during and immediately following this festival of harvest. The Feast of Pentecost was truly a time of exceptional spiritual harvest. As a result of Peter's sermon on the day of Pentecost, "about three thousand were added to their number that day" (Acts 2:41). In the days following Pentecost "many who heard the message believed, and the number of men grew to about five thousand" (Acts 4:4). Within the first four chapters of the Acts of the Apostles, the church increased from the 120 gathered in the Upper Room to 5,000 throughout Jerusalem—an astonishing growth rate of 4,167%!

God's revelation to Moses on Mount Sinai was certainly also on the minds of the disciples, when "suddenly a sound like the blowing of a violent wind came from heaven and filled the whole house where they were sitting" (Acts 2:2). This time, the turbulent elements were not heralding the Law, but the long awaited Lawyer—the Paraclete—the One who would serve as every believer's Advocate (John 16:16, 26; 1 John 2:1). By definition, the Paraclete (from the Greek word *parakletos*) is "a legal assistant, advocate or intercessor." The Law imparted on Mount Sinai condemned and was impossible to keep. The Divine Advocate poured out at Pentecost, the Holy Spirit himself, bestowed strength, direction, comfort and victory to those who have been "set … free from the law of sin and death" (Romans 8:2).

Christ's Sanctifying Mission

Was Pentecost, like Passover, Unleavened Bread and Firstfruits, also a prophetic archetype? The New Testament makes it exceedingly clear that Pentecost too found its meaning and fulfillment in Christ's sanctifying mission of redemption.

During the Feast of Pentecost, the two loaves brought into the Temple (Leviticus 23:17) represented two facts—one historical, the other theological. Historically, the two loaves represented the double portion of manna God provided the day before each Sabbath while the Children of Israel wandered in the wilderness. Theologically, the two loaves represented Jew and Gentile. With the coming of the Holy Spirit, Christ's mission was completed. Writing to the Ephesian church, Paul concisely expressed this truth:

> For he [Jesus] himself is our peace, who has made the two [Jew and Gentile] one and has destroyed the barrier, the dividing wall of hostility, by abolishing in his flesh the law with its commandments and regulations. His purpose was to create in himself one new man out of the two, thus making peace, and in this one body to reconcile both of them to God through the cross, by which he put to death their hostility (Ephesians 2:14-16).

"Leaven" remains in both loaves—Jews and Gentiles—for Christ has not yet come to glorify his church. During this time of waiting, sin remains within the church. The leaven persists. However, when the Messiah, our "unleavened" Bridegroom, returns for his Bride, the church, we will become like him. We will then be his "radiant church, without stain or wrinkle or any other blemish, but holy and blameless" (Ephesians 5:27).

The Gospel Illustrated

In the final, momentous year of Jesus' earthly ministry, the first four feasts found their consummation in his life: He was crucified on Passover, buried on the Feast of Unleavened Bread, raised on the Feast of Firstfruits, and he sent the Holy Spirit, "another Counselor" (John 14:16) on Pentecost. Explaining away these marked parallels as coincidence would be absurd. By Divine design, the festivals explain and illustrate the foundational truths of the Gospel.

Since the church has not yet witnessed the consummate fulfillment of the fifth feast, the Feast of Trumpets (see chapter 6), we remain under the principle of Pentecost, i.e., continuing "the summer cultivation" under the direction and power of the

Holy Spirit. During this long period of harvest, we must continually remember Jesus' admonition: "The harvest is plentiful but the workers are few. Ask the Lord of the harvest, therefore, to send out workers into his harvest field" (Matthew 9:37-38).

The experience of Pentecost continues to be the great need of the church today. With the prophetic discernment of a modern patriarch, Billy Graham laments:

> *Everywhere I go, I find that God's people lack something. God's people are hungry for something; God's people are thirsting for something ... The Church today is powerless ... We have no power because we do not have the Spirit of God in power and in fullness, in our lives. The Bible says, "Be filled with the Spirit" (Ephesians 5:18).*[1]

Pentecost, a feast and an experience; a reminder of the past and an annual summons to fulfill the Great Commission (Matthew 28:18-20). Jesus said:

> *Wait for the gift my Father promised ... you will receive power when the Holy Spirit comes on you; and you will be my witnesses in Jerusalem, and in all Judea and Samaria, and to the ends of the earth (Acts 1:4,8).*

Believers must continue diligently to witness and work, through the enabling power of the Holy Spirit, patiently awaiting the fulfillment of the next feast. As James Milton Black graphically describes it in his well–loved gospel song, we look forward to the day "when the trumpet of the Lord will sound, and time will be no more..."[2]

---

[1] Quoted from the sermon, "How to Be Filled with the Spirit," printed in *Revival in Our Time* published by the Van Kampen Press.

[2] *The Song Book of The Salvation Army* (Verona, NJ: The Salvation Army, 1987), no. 907, p. 252

... *To Ponder*

• Read: Acts 1

1. The key verse in the Book of Acts, and also its outline, is found in Acts 1:8. Write a free translation of this verse in your own words.

2. What were the disciples told to do in anticipation of this promise? (Acts 1:4)

• Read: Acts 2

3. On the Shavuot morning described in Acts 2, God confirmed the establishment of a new covenant with Israel as the prophets had foretold. List the characteristics of the new covenant described in the following Old Testament prophecies:

    a.   Isaiah 59:19-21 _____

    _____

    b.   Jeremiah 31:31-34 _____

    _____

    c.   Joel 2:28-32 _____

    _____

4. Beside the 120 gathered in the upper room at Pentecost, who else was specifically said to have been filled with the Spirit? Note those involved and the circumstances according to the following references?

    a. Acts 4:8   _____

    b. Acts 4:31   _____

    c. Acts 6:3   _____

    d. Acts 6:5   _____

    e. Acts 7:55   _____

    f. Acts 9:17   _____

    g. Acts 11:24 _____

    h. Acts 13:9   _____

    i. Acts 13:52 _____

5. What does the phrase "filled with the Holy Spirit mean to you?"

Chapter 6

Rosh Hashanna— New Year

Beneath the iridescent dome
The shofar sounds,
Reverberates,
Shocking the eardrums of memory,
Focusing the mind.
Black–frocked men rock
In timeless rhythm,
Smooth undulations,
A ceaseless paean of faith
Striking melancholy chords
To internal music.

     —*Joyce B. Schwartz*

The LORD said to Moses, "Say to
the Israelites: 'On the first day of the
seventh month you are to have a day
of rest, a sacred assembly commemorated with trumpet blasts. Do no
regular work, but present an offering made to the LORD by fire.'"
    — *Leviticus 23:23-25*

*A*fter the long summer following the Feast of Pentecost comes the seventh month. The three concluding festivals set forth in Leviticus 23 represent the final work of redemption: the Feast of Trumpets, the Day of Atonement and the Feast of Tabernacles.

In many contexts throughout Scripture, the number seven has distinct, symbolic meaning. Since God took seven days to create the universe, seven connotes completion, culmination, finality. It is therefore no surprise that holy days in the seventh month of the Jewish calendar, Tishri (September), focus on God's complete and final work for his creation.

The three fall feasts conclude the annual cycle of the celebrations ordered by God in Leviticus 23. Individually, each feast speaks of completion and beginning—the end of the old, the beginning of the new. Collectively, the trilogy augments and completes the essential historic and prophetic truths illustrated by each festival.

The following list shows the close chronological relationship of the fall feasts:

Tishri (September–October)

1	Rosh Hashanna
2–9	Days of Awe (including Rosh Hashanna)
10–14	Yom Kippur (Day of Atonement)
15–21	Sukkot (Feast of Tabernacles)
22	Shemini Atzeret (Eighth Day of Assembly)

Beginning of the Year

The Feast of Trumpets, known in the Hebrew Bible as *Zikhron Teruah* ("Memorial of Blowing"—Leviticus 23:24) and *Yom Teruah* ("Day of Blowing"—Numbers 29:1) is now commonly called *Rosh Hashanna*, literally, "head of the year." Before Second Temple times (before the fifth century B.C.), the new year clearly originated on 1 Nisan. Jewish tradition therefore understands Rosh Hashanna to be the inauguration of the civil new year, since it is the anniversary of the world's creation—the birthday of the world!

New Years Day for the Jews is not just a holiday; it is a holy day as well. Rosh Hashanna, together with the Day of Atonement, are known as the "days of awe." It is not a time for levity, but for contemplation and prayer. It is a solemn period when Jews believe that all people stand before their Creator.

Blowing of the Shofar

The Lord designated this day for the blowing of the trumpets. He seems to have favored the trumpet, or *shofar* ("ram's horn"). Harking back to the time God spared Isaac's life by means of a ram caught in the thicket by its horn, the ram's horn became a symbol of redemption, renewal and rejoicing.

Trumpets symbolized Israel's return to the land of their fathers and the regathering that would result in Israel's acceptance of the Messiah. Isaiah heralded the forecast:

> You, O Israelites, will be gathered up one by one. And in that day a great trumpet will sound. Those who were perishing in Assyria and those who were exiled in Egypt will come and worship the LORD on the holy mountain in Jerusalem (Isaiah 27:12-13).

The New Testament also pictures the trumpet as ushering in the Rapture. The apostle Paul reminds believers that they will be gathered into heaven with the sound of the trumpet (1 Thessalonians 4:16-17).

Today, the ritual most frequently associated with Rosh

Hashanna is the sounding of the shofar in the synagogue. According to Jewish tradition, a person who has not listened to the shofar has not observed the day. Just listening to the shofar means obedience to one of God's 248 positive commandments found in the Torah (or Pentateuch—the first five books of the Bible). The rabbis pressed the point further, contending that it is not enough to hear the shofar by accident. The hearer must listen with the *kavanah* (intention) of fulfilling the biblical commandment.

According to the Mishnah (second century codification of the Oral Law), the shofar of the Temple in Jerusalem was different from the others used on Rosh Hashanna. It was plated with gold. Other shofars were used for specified events. For example, during times of distress, such as war or a fast proclaimed due to the lack of rain, a silver–plated shofar was sounded.

Three basic trumpet calls reverberate in the synagogue during the Rosh Hashanna service. First is the *t'kiyah*—one long, sustained blast. In ancient Israel, this was a reassuring sound. It signified that the watchman was on duty, and all was well.

The second call comprises three successive blasts of equal length known as *shevarim*. In biblical times *shevarim* was sounded for a significant event—the arrival of an important visitor or the proclamation of good news.

The third trumpet call, however, is a dour warning. It is the call for alarm. Referred to as *t'ruah*, it consists of nine rapid blasts on the shofar. Some believe that this was the call used by the "seven priests carrying the seven trumpets … marching before the ark of the LORD and blowing the trumpets" (Joshua 6.13) in the final divine maneuver to conquer Jericho.

Indeed, Rosh Hashanna is the Day of Alarm. It is a reminder that although the summer harvest season has ended, and the storehouses are full, each person must recognize his sole dependency on God; not on himself (see Deuteronomy 8:10-14).

On This Day

According to Jewish tradition, it was on Rosh Hashanna that ...

- God completed creation by creating Adam and Eve (Genesis 1:27).
- God banished Adam and Eve from the Garden of Eden (Genesis 3:23).
- Cain and Abel were born (Genesis 4:1-2), each with a twin sister.
- Cain attacked and killed his brother Abel (Genesis 4:8).
- Cain and his father, Adam, repented of their respective sins, and God forgave them.
- In the days of the great Flood, the waters began to recede (Genesis 8:1).
- Sarah, Rachel and Hannah conceived (Genesis 21:2; Genesis 25:21; 1 Samuel 1:20).
- At age 137, Abraham took his 37-year-old son, Isaac, to be sacrificed on Mount Moriah (Genesis 22:3).
- Sarah, Abraham's wife, died (Genesis 23:1-2).
- Rebecca, wife of Isaac, died (Genesis 49:31).
- Joseph was freed from Pharaoh's prison (Genesis 41:39-4).

Heralding the Rapture

While Rosh Hashanna prophesies and celebrates the regathering of Israel to the Promised Land, for the follower of

Christ it also looks forward to the Rapture—Christ's second coming. As with the sounding of the shofar, believers await the final trumpet call. Until then ...

- We *rejoice* with the apostle Paul:
For the Lord himself will come down from heaven, with a loud command, with the voice of the archangel and with the trumpet call of God, and the dead in Christ will rise first. After that, we who are still alive and are left will be caught up together with them in the clouds to meet the Lord in the air. And so we will be with the Lord forever (1 Thessalonians 4:16-17).

- We *anticipate* with the poet Henry Vaughan:
Let my course, my aim, my love,
And chief acquaintance be above;
So when that day and hour shall come,
In which Thyself shall be the sun,
Thou'lt find me drest and on my way,
Watching the break of Thy great day.[1]

- We *petition* with the apostle John:
He who testifies to these things says, 'Yes, I am coming soon.' Amen. Come, Lord Jesus (Revelation 22:20).

---

[1] Henry Vaughan, "The Dawning," in *Handbook of Preaching Resources from English Literature*, ed. James Douglas Robertson (New York: The Macmillan Company, 1962), 14.

...*To Ponder*

• Read: Nehemiah 8:1-12

1. The Book of Nehemiah records the observance of Rosh
Hashanna following Judah's return from captivity in Babylon.
The remnant that returned to Israel assembled "on the first
day of the seventh month" (8:2).

   a. Ezra read the Law to the assembly in the square near
   the _____ Gate.

   b. He read the Law from _____ to
   _____.

   c. When Ezra praised the Lord, the people responded
   "_____" and "_____."

   d. As they listened to the words of the Law, the people
   _____.

   e. Nehemiah declared, "This day is sacred to our Lord.
   Do not grieve, _____
   _____."

• Read: Joel 2:1-3:21

2. Joel's sweeping portrayal of the implications of the Feast
of Trumpets introduces specific themes. Joel reveals that Israel
is moving toward her historic day of regathering. Give a title to
each division of the prophet's forecast:

   a. 2:1-14 _____

   b. 2:15-17 _____

c.　2:18-32 _____

d.　3:1-11 _____

e.　3:12-15 _____

f.　3:16 _____

g.　3:17-21 _____

• Read: Isaiah 27:12-13

3.　Reflect on Isaiah's prophecy concerning Israel's national return to the land of their fathers.

Chapter 7

Yom Kippur—
Day of Atonement

Behold! the blest Redeemer comes,
 Th' eternal Son appears,
And, at th'appointed time, assumes
 The body God prepares.

No blood of beasts, on altars shed,
 Could wash the conscience clean;
But the rich sacrifice He paid
 Atones for all our sin.
                    —Isaac Watts

The LORD *said to Moses, "The tenth day of this seventh month is the Day of Atonement. Hold a sacred assembly and deny yourselves, and present an offering made to the* LORD *by fire."*

—*Leviticus 23:26-27*

*T*he Day of Atonement (*Yom Kippur*) fell exactly ten days after the Feast of Trumpets (*Rosh Hashanna*). Unlike the other Feasts of the Lord, Yom Kippur was not a time of feasting. It was a national fast day. On this annual day of humiliation and expiation for the sins of the nation, the high priest offered sacrifices as an atonement for the priests and the people. Detailed instructions for the observance are found in Leviticus 16, 23:26-32 and Numbers 29:7-11.

We find this somber day of repentance summarized in Leviticus 16:29-33:

> *This is to be a lasting ordinance for you: On the tenth day of the seventh month you must deny yourselves and not do any work—whether native-born or an alien living among you—because on this day atonement will be made for you, to cleanse you. Then, before the Lord, you will be clean from all your sins. It is a sabbath of rest, and you must deny yourselves; it is a lasting ordinance. The priest who is anointed and ordained to succeed his father as high priest is to make atonement. He is to put on the sacred linen garments and make atonement for the Most Holy Place, for the Tent of Meeting and the altar, and for the priests and all the people of the community.*

The High Priest

In the days of the Temple, responsibility for Yom Kippur focused on the high priest. His arduous duties on this day were extraordinarily complicated. Literally every step the bare-footed high priest took in the Court, Sanctuary and Holy of Holies was meticulously scripted. According to the Babylonian Talmud (*Tractate Yoma*) the high priest made forty-two trips between the Court and the Sanctuary on this spectacular day.

To fulfill his many duties, the high priest began to prepare himself a week before the Day of Atonement. Daily sequestered in the *Palhedrin* (the high priest's chamber) in the Temple Courts, he studiously examined the laws relating to Yom Kippur. Simultaneously, another priest prepared himself in similar fashion in case anything unforeseen happened to the high priest that would disqualify him from officiating on this sacred day.

Since this was the awesome day of judgment, the high priest could not make a mistake. An error, a miscalculation, could be costly. While a mistake might mean the life of the high priest, it could also signify that there would be no atonement for that year.

In fulfillment of the requirements of the Torah, the high priest wore eight garments on the Day of Atonement: 1) the golden crown on his forehead, 2) the breastplate upon his heart, 3) the outer robe decorated with bells, 4) the apron, or vest. Besides these high priestly garments, on this day he would also wear four garments made from white flax normally worn by ordinary priests. They include: 5) the robe, 6) the belt, 7) the turban and 8) pants. The high priest changed back and forth several times throughout the day between his "golden garments" and his "white garments."

Throughout the day the people could hear the golden bells on the hem of the high priest's garments. Each time he changed garments, a linen cloth separated him from the people. They could not see him, but they could hear the assuring tinkle of the tiny bells, and they knew that they had a living high priest!

During the course of the services, the high priest voiced the Tetragrammaton (*YHWH* "Yahweh"—the sacred, ordinarily unutterable, name for God) a total of ten times. The Day of Atonement was the only occasion when this most holy name was spoken. When the people heard the high priest say the

Jerusalem's glistening Dome of the Rock has changed little since its construction 1300 years ago. It sits on or near the site of the Temple built by Solomon, reconstructed by Zerubbabel, and remodeled by Herod the Great.

"I rejoiced with those who said to me, 'Let us go to the house of the LORD.' Our feet are standing in your gates, O Jerusalem. Jerusalem is built like a city that is closely compacted together. That is where the tribes go up, the tribes of the LORD, to praise the name of the LORD according to the statute given to Israel." —from a Psalm of Ascents (Psalm 122:1–4)

Above: The western wall of the Temple Mount is considered a synagogue and is therefore a place for studying the Torah and discussing theology.

Right: A Hasidic ("pious, righteous") Jew and his son pray at the Western Wall. Since the destruction of the Temple by the Romans in 70 A.D., Jews have come here to pray, express their grief over the destroyed Temple and their hope for its restoration upon the Messiah's coming.

"After three days they found [Jesus] in the temple courts, sitting among the teachers, listening to them and asking them questions. Everyone who heard him was amazed at his understanding and his answers."

—Luke 2:46-47

"And [Jesus] said to them, 'I have eagerly desired to eat this Passover with you before I suffer. For I tell you, I will not eat it again until it finds fulfillment in the kingdom of God.'" —Luke 22:15-16

The "Blessing of the Priests" conducted during Passover at the Western Wall in Jerusalem.

During the Seder, the leader takes the middle matzah from the three-sectioned special covering called a *matzah tash* (linen bag) and breaks it in two. Half is returned to the middle section between the two whole matzas. The other half, called the *afikomen*, is wrapped in a linen cloth and hidden. Later in the ritual the children find and redeem the *afikomen*.

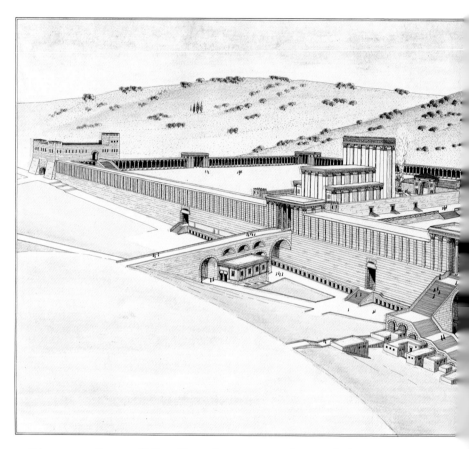

Ritmeyer, Leen. "The Temple Mount of Herod the Great" (No. 32). Skelton England: Ritmeyer Archaelogical Design.

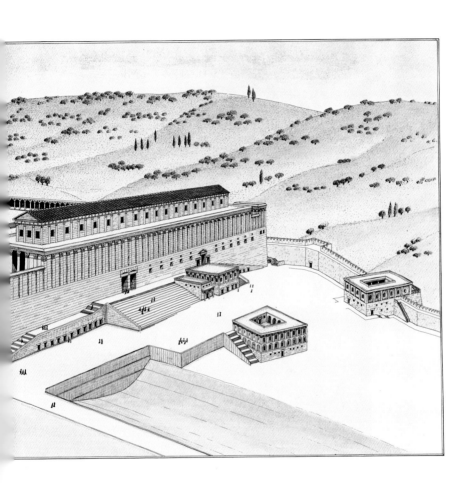

Rabbi Judah Kogen welcomes Lt. Colonels William and Marilyn Francis to the Congregation Sons of Israel's (Suffern, New York) *Sukkah* during the Feast of Tabernacles.

"Then the survivors from all the nations that have attacked Jerusalem will go up year after year to worship the King, the LORD Almighty, and to celebrate the Feast of Tabernacles."   —*Zechariah 14:16*

The Mount of Olives as viewed from across the Kidron Valley. The Church of All Nations (center) in the Garden of Gethsemane sits at the foot of the mountain, directly east of the Temple Mount. The Mount of Olives and adjoining hills abundantly supplied the required flora for celebrating the Feast of Tabernacles.

The Temple in Jesus' day as reconstructed in the model of first century Jerusalem located on the grounds of the Holyland Hotel. During the Feast of Tabernacles, the Levite choir sang selected portions of scripture on the fifteen steps leading up to the Nieanor Doors separating the Court of the Women and the Court of the Israelites.

"The land of Israel is at the center of the world; Jerusalem is at the center of the land of Israel; the Temple is at the center of Jerusalem ..."   —*Midrash Tanhuma: Kedoshim 10*

Stephen Katz sounds the *shofar*, or ram's horn, on Rosh Hashanna for the Congregation Sons of Israel (Suffern, New York). The view of Jerusalem from the Mount of Olives is the background.

"And in that day a great trumpet will sound. Those who were perishing in Assyria and those who were exiled in Egypt will come and worship the LORD on the holy mountain in Jerusalem." —Isaiah 27:13

word *YHWH*, the entire congregation groaned in unison and fell prostrate on the ground in reverence and awe.

The day began at dawn when an appointed priest would declare: "Go out (to the roof of the Temple) and see if the time for the sacrifice has arrived." If the sun had arisen, the priest cried out, "The day has dawned!" With this announcement, the high priest ceremoniously purified himself with the first of five immersions throughout the day.

Two Goats for Sacrifice

One of the high priest's first duties was to make his own confession in the area between the Temple and the altar. The high priest then went to the north side of the altar with an assistant at his right and the head of the priestly family at his left. In front of the party stood two goats with their heads toward the Temple and their backs toward the people. Both goats must have been purchased for the same price and be identical in size and appearance.

A golden lottery box, designed especially for this ceremony, was placed on the stone pavement nearby. The box contained two golden tablets. They were identical, except one bore the name "For YHWH" (meaning, for the service of God) and the other, "For Azazel" (the scapegoat). The high priest shook the box. With a dramatic, singular motion, he thrust both hands in and withdrew one tablet in each hand. He then placed each lot on the head of the respective goat.

It was considered a favorable sign if the tablet marked "For YHWH" emerged in the priest's right hand. When this happened, the high priest's assistant would declare, "My master, the high priest! Raise up your right hand!"

The high priest fastened one piece of scarlet cloth to the

horn of the goat for Azazel, the scapegoat, and another around
the neck of the goat to be slain for YHWH. He then turned the
scapegoat to face the congregation. There the goat would wait
until the sins of the people were laid on it, and the scapegoat
would convey them "to a solitary place" (Leviticus 16:22).

The high priest then sacrificed a young bull as his "own
sin offering to make atonement for himself and his household"
(Leviticus 16:11). The bull's blood flowed into a basin, and a
priest continually stirred it so that it would not coagulate.

The high priest entered the Holy of Holies for the first time
that day, initially placing a censer of burning coals on the "foundation stone." He entered again for a second time with the
blood of the young bull, sprinkling the blood toward the place
where the Ark of the Covenant had rested in the First Temple
(1 Kings 8:3-8). Emerging from the Holy of Holies, the high
priest cautiously placed the bowl of blood in front of the
Temple's veil.

Now it was time to sacrifice the goat chosen by lot "For
YHWH." Entering the Holy of Holies for the third time, he
ceremoniously cleansed the sanctuary with the sacrificial blood.

The Scapegoat

All this time, the scapegoat stood facing the people. Robed
in white, the high priest placed both his hands upon the scapegoat and proceeded to "confess over it all the wickedness and
rebellion of the Israelites—all their sins—and put them on the
goat's head" (Leviticus 16:21).

A priest led the goat over the Mount of Olives to a predetermined site outside the city limits. Along the ten–mile journey he read the Torah and rested at temporary stands constructed for this purpose. Someone was waiting at each loca-

The Second Temple

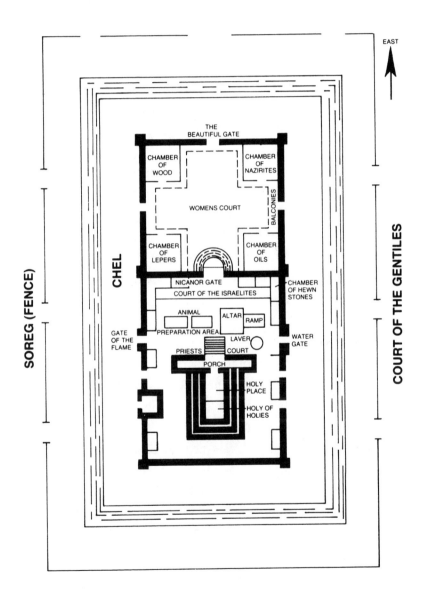

tion to escort the priest and goat to the next stop. After the last stand, the priest and goat walked alone to the edge of a cliff.

At the edge of the precipice, the priest removed the scarlet ribbon from the goat's horns and divided it in two. He retied one strand to the horns and attached the other to the cliff. The scapegoat was then forced over the precipice, thus paying the ultimate sacrifice—"For the life of a creature is in the blood ... it is the blood that makes atonement for one's life" (Leviticus 17:11). According to tradition, the scarlet cloth around the scapegoat's horns turned white upon its death in keeping with the promise of Isaiah 1:18: "Though your sins are like scarlet, they shall be as white as snow; though they are red as crimson, they shall be like wool."

The news that the scapegoat had died "outside the camp," was swiftly returned to the high priest who, with immense relief, bathed and changed his garments.

A Better Hope

The significant irony of the Day of Atonement was that the more accurately the letter of the Law was obeyed, the more it graphically illustrated that the Law itself was "weak and useless (for the law made nothing perfect), and a better hope is introduced, by which we draw near to God" (Hebrews 7:18-19). This "better hope" is the One who has become the final and perfect Scapegoat—Jesus Christ.

We can envision no more explicit type of the Messiah than that of him who was presented to Pilate. As did the scapegoat, Jesus quietly stood in front of the crowd before he was led away to "the place of the Skull" (John 19:17) carrying the sins of the world. In the words of the apostle Paul: "God presented him as a sacrifice of atonement, through faith in his blood" (Romans 3:25).

Beside being heralded as the sacrifice of atonement, Christ is also characterized as our high priest. The writer to the Hebrews presents this truth in context and perspective:

> *When Christ came as high priest of the good things that are already here, he went through the greater and more perfect tabernacle that is not man–made, that is to say, not a part of this creation. He did not enter by means of the blood of goats and calves; but he entered the Most Holy Place once for all by his own blood, having obtained eternal redemption. The blood of goats and bulls and the ashes of a heifer sprinkled on those who are ceremonially unclean sanctify them so that they are outwardly clean. How much more, then, will the blood of Christ, who through the eternal Spirit offered himself unblemished to God, cleanse our consciences from acts that lead to death, so that we may serve the living God! (Hebrews 9:11-14)*

For the author of the book of Hebrews, the Day of Atonement illustrates that all the sacrifices of the Law cannot affect the problems of forgiveness and atonement. Only Jesus Christ, our eternal High Priest, can say, "I give them eternal life, and they shall never perish" (John 10:28). The Levitical sacrifices were but "a shadow of the good things that are coming, not the realities themselves. For this reason it can never, by the same sacrifices repeated endlessly year after year, make perfect those who draw near to worship" (Hebrews 10:1-2).

A Future Day of Atonement

The rituals and sacrifices of the Day of Atonement carry rich prophetic truth. While Jesus already has fulfilled his initial function as both the eternal High Priest and Scapegoat, he will come again. A future Day of Atonement will follow the Rapture of the believers. The High Priest will again leave the Holy of Holies in the heavens and return, clothed in robes of righteousness. The prophet Zechariah looks forward to this day:

> On that day I will set out to destroy all the nations that attack Jerusalem. And I will pour out on the house of David and the inhabitants of Jerusalem a spirit of grace and supplication. They will look on me, the one they have pierced, and they will mourn for him as one mourns for an only child, and grieve bitterly for him as one grieves for a firstborn son. On that day the weeping in Jerusalem will be great ... (Zechariah 12:9-11).

This is the Tribulation period that will serve as Israel's great Day of Atonement. On that day, the nations of the world will remember the veracity and fulfillment of Isaiah's prophecy:

> He was despised and rejected by men, a man of sorrows, and familiar with suffering. Like one from whom men hide their faces he was despised, and we esteemed him not.
> Surely he took up our infirmities and carried our sorrows, yet we considered him stricken by God, smitten by him, and afflicted. But he was pierced for our transgressions, he was crushed for our iniquities; the punishment that brought us peace was upon him, and by his wounds we are healed. We all, like sheep, have gone astray, each of us has turned to his own way; and the Lord has laid on him the iniquity of us all.
> He was oppressed and afflicted, yet he did not open his mouth; he was led like a lamb to the slaughter, and as a sheep before her shearers is silent, so he did not open his mouth. By oppression and judgment he was taken away. And who can speak of his descendants? For he was cut off from the land of the living; for the transgression of my people he was stricken. He was assigned a grave with the wicked, and with the rich in

his death, though he had done no violence, nor was any deceit in his mouth.

Yet it was the LORD's will to crush him and cause him to suffer, and though the LORD makes his life a guilt offering, he will see his offspring and prolong his days, and the will of the LORD will prosper in his hand. After the suffering of his soul, he will see the light of life and be satisfied; by his knowledge my righteous servant will justify many, and he will bear their iniquities. Therefore I will give him a portion among the great, and he will divide the spoils with the strong, because he poured out his life unto death, and was numbered with the transgressors. For he bore the sin of many, and made intercession for the transgressors (Isaiah 53:3-12).

From Mourning to Celebration

The gladsome Feast of Tabernacles follows the awesome days of mourning. As the renowned nineteenth century preacher Charles Spurgeon observed, "Sacred sorrow prepares the heart for holy joy. We must receive the atonement before we can enter the joy of the Lord."[1]

---

[1] Charles Haddon Spurgeon, *Spurgeon's Devotional Bible* (Grand Rapids, Mich.: Baker Book House, 1977), 110.

...*To Ponder*

• Read: Leviticus 16:1-34

1. As you read the description of the Day of Atonement in Leviticus 16, list the spiritual principles you see in its observance.

• Read: Hebrews 7:11-28

2. Why was the Law "weak and useless" (7:18) and "only a shadow of the good things that are coming—not the realities themselves" (10:1)?

3. The writer of Hebrews states that "because Jesus lives forever" he is our eternal high priest (7:24). List the characteristics that qualify Jesus to be our high priest (7:26-28).

• Read: Hebrews 9:11-14

Undergirding the theology of this passage are three basic truths: 1) Humanity's fundamental need is access to the Creator; 2) This is a world of dim shadows and imperfect copies of reality and 3) There can be no salvation without sacrifice.

4. How does Christ relate to and fulfill each of these three theological axioms?

• Read: Hebrews 9:22-24

5. Try to image the blood of Christ as a witness in heaven. What does the concept of the blood add to your understanding of heaven?

• Read: Hebrews 10:1-18

6. The writer to the Hebrews was not saying anything new when he said that obedience was the only true sacrifice (10:8-9). This truth is a prominent theme of Scripture (see Isaiah 1:11-20 and Micah 6:6-8). Write your personal translation of the following verses:

    a. 1 Samuel 15:22

    b. Psalm 50:14

    c. Psalm 51:16-17

    d. Hosea 6:6

Chapter 8

Sukkot—Tabernacles

Then the survivors from all the nations that have attacked Jerusalem will go up year after year to worship the King, the Lord Almighty, and to celebrate the Feast of Tabernacles …

On that day Holy to the Lord will be inscribed on the bells of the horses, and the cooking pots in the Lord's house will be like the sacred bowls in front of the altar. Every pot in Jerusalem and Judah will be holy to the Lord Almighty, and all who come to sacrifice will take some of the pots and cook in them. And on that day there will no longer be a Canaanite in the house of the Lord Almighty.

—*Zechariah 14:16, 20-21*

The LORD said to Moses, "Say to the Israelites: 'On the fifteenth day of the seventh month the LORD's Feast of Tabernacles begins, and it lasts for seven days. The first day is a sacred assembly; do no regular work. For seven days present offerings made to the LORD by fire, and on the eighth day hold a sacred assembly and present an offering made to the LORD by fire. It is the closing assembly; do no regular work.'"

—Leviticus 23:33-36

*I*srael's great fall feasts span the range of human emotion—the solemn contemplation of the Feast of Trumpets (*Rosh Hashanna*), the dread and apprehension of the Day of Atonement (*Yom Kippur)* and the triumph and jubilation of the Feast of Tabernacles (*Sukkot).*

While the Feasts of the Lord contain historical, agricultural, sacrificial and prophetic characteristics, the fall sequence holds extensive prophetic significance. Rosh Hashanna looks forward to Israel's return to the land of their fathers (Isaiah 27:12-13). Yom Kippur foreshadows the day of Israel's final repentance and reconciliation (Zechariah 12:10-13:1). The climactic Feast of Tabernacles forecasts the nation's final restoration under the rule of the Messiah (Zechariah 14:16-19).

The Feast for Every Nation

The Feast of Tabernacles is known by several names: the Feast of Booths (Leviticus 23:42), the Feast of Ingathering (Exodus 23:16) and the Feast of Sukkot (1 Kings 8:2). This feast, celebrated in the Hebrew month of Tishri (September–October), gained such prominence that people frequently called it simply "the Feast" (John 7:37). "The Feast" is the usual designation for Sukkot in the Talmud (see also 1 Kings 8:2 and Deuteronomy 16:14). The English word "tabernacle" is derived from the Latin *tabernaculum* meaning "booth" or "shed." It acquired this name from God's requirement for all the Israelites to dwell in temporary shelters (booths, tabernacles) during the seven-day celebration.

The Feast of Tabernacles was the final harvest festival, a feast accompanied with great joy and thanksgiving for God's provision. God commanded his people to "Celebrate the Feast of Tabernacles for seven days ... Be joyful at your Feast"

(Deuteronomy 16:13-14).

Sukkot heralds a time when believers of *every* nation will one day come to Jerusalem to celebrate the feast during the Messiah's reign. At that millennial festival, the world will worship God as Creator, Preserver and Governor of all things.

According to Numbers 29:12-32, seventy bulls were sacrificed during the Feast of Tabernacles. The Jewish sages believed that these bulls represented the nations of the world (*Sukkah 55b*). Indeed, the Scripture declares that one day all nations will acknowledge YAHWEH as Lord:

> *The Lord will be king over the whole earth. On that day there will be one Lord, and his name the only name (Zechariah 14:9).*

Even the nations that have made war against Israel will honor the King of Kings and Lord of Lords. Zechariah goes on to declare:

> *Then the survivors from all the nations that have attacked Jerusalem will go up year after year to worship the King, the Lord Almighty, and to celebrate the Feast of Tabernacles … The Lord will bring on them the plague he inflicts on the nations that do not go up to celebrate the Feast of Tabernacles. This will be the punishment to Egypt and the punishment of all the nations that do not go up to celebrate the Feast of Tabernacles (Zechariah 14:16-19).*

The Celebration

To celebrate this joyous festival, God instructed his people to live in a temporary dwelling called *Sukkah* (meaning, "booth") for seven days. In doing so, they would remember and commemorate the Exodus when their ancestors lived in tents on their journey to the Promised Land (Leviticus 23:41-43). The temporary structures must be open to the elements. Through the booth's flimsy frame one must see the sky and remember that God is his or her sole source of peace and security.

God instructed that four types of branches must be used throughout the celebration:

> On the first day you are to take choice fruit from the trees, and palm fronds, leafy branches and poplars, and rejoice before the LORD your God for seven days (Leviticus 23:40).

While the Mount of Olives and adjoining hills supplied these required flora in abundance, specific identification of each species became a matter of tradition. The conventional items used include: the *Etrog*, a sweet fragrant citrus, for the "boughs of goodly trees"; the *Lulav*, branches of a palm tree with elongated leaves, for the "branches of palm trees"; the *Hadas*, myrtle twigs covered with leaves, three at a time from the same level on the stem, for the "boughs of thick trees," and the *Aravah*, shoots of willow with long leaves and red stems, for the "willows of the brook."

Rejoicing over the goodness of God, the entire congregation waved these branches before the Lord throughout the seven days. The Four Species and the Sukkah are the abiding symbols of this distinctive festival. Both signs remind the worshiper of God's constant provision for his people throughout the ages. Sukkot was consequently the festival of unrestrained jubilation.

Although not specifically commanded by God, a ritual of offering a water libation became part of the daily temple liturgy. The rabbis contend that "he who has not seen the celebration of drawing water (on the Feast of Tabernacles) has

Jerusalem in 30 A.D.

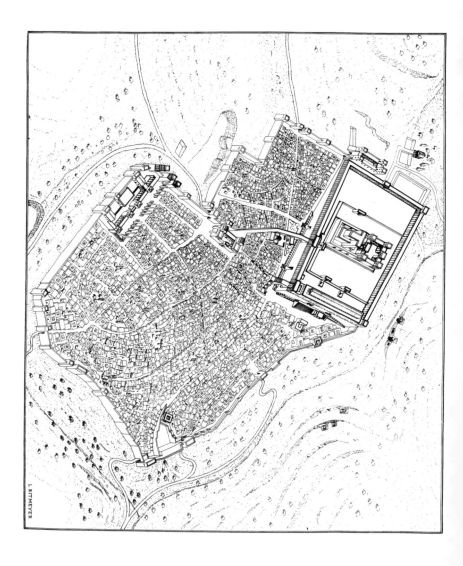

never experienced true joy in his life" (*Mishna Tractate Sukka* chapter 5).

The Water–Libation Ceremony

Every morning of the feast a priest walked down to the Pool of Siloam, just south of the Temple Mount. He ceremoniously filled a large golden pitcher with the pool's clear, cold water. Retracing his steps the quarter mile up to the Temple, he entered through the Hulda Gates to the attending blast of silver trumpets. As the priest passed by, the celebrants chanted various biblical texts, including Isaiah 12:3—"With joy you will draw water from the wells of salvation."

When the priest reached the altar, he received a container of wine, and ascended the ramp with the Siloam water in one hand and the wine in the other. Standing over the altar, he poured both elements into separate silver vessels that hung over the altar. Throughout the ceremony, Levites sang hymns while standing on the fifteen steps leading up to the giant Nicanor Doors in the Court of the Women. During the pouring of the wine and water, they prayed for the entire congregation —"O Lord, save us; O Lord, grant us success" (Psalm 118:25).

The daily water libation symbolized:

- A *memorial* to God for his provision in the desert
- A *prayer* that God would again give water for the next harvest
- A *forecast* of the days of the Messiah

Jesus Attends the Feast

The apostle John records the gripping account of the last time Jesus journeyed to Jerusalem for the Feast of Tabernacles (John 7:1-10:21). It was about six months before his crucifixion. Jesus used this festival of Sukkot to declare three of the eight *I Am* pronouncements recorded in the Gospel of John (John 8:12, 10:7, 10:11) and to heal a man who was blind from birth (John 9). In addition, he stunned the priests and Levites on the seventh and final day of the feast with an astonishing claim (John 7:37-44).

Jesus arrived at the feast in disguise. He had previously told his disciples that he would not attend the feast (John 7:6-9), but changed his mind: "after his brothers had left for the Feast, he went also, not publicly, but in secret" (John 7:10). He remained in disguise until halfway (three or four days) through the feast, when he went "up to the temple courts and (began) to teach" (John 7:14).

On the last day of the feast, *Hoshana Raba* ("the great day of the call for help"), Jesus interrupted the morning water libation with a shocking claim. While the biblical record does not specify the exact moment Jesus shouted his seemingly preposterous claim, it may have occurred as the priest carried the golden pitcher of water past him in the temple courts.

John records the confrontation: "On the last and greatest day of the Feast, Jesus stood and said in a loud voice, 'If anyone is thirsty, let him come to me and drink. Whoever believes in me, as the Scripture has said, streams of living water will flow from within him'" (John 7:37-38).

With these contentious, penetrating words, Jesus launched the final phase of his ministry, that of direct confrontation with the religious authorities. John notes that "the people were divided ... Some wanted to seize him, but no one laid a hand on him" (John 7:43-44). Later that day, the authorities "picked up stones to stone him, but Jesus hid himself, slipping away from the temple grounds" (John 8:59).

Jesus' final pilgrimage to the Feast of Tabernacles underscored and expanded the meaning of Sukkot. Jesus was the living testimony to God's love for all people. He alone was the vital, spiritual, eternal water of life. He indeed was the long-awaited Messiah!

The Messiah's Return

The prophecies depicted by the Feast of Tabernacles will be fulfilled when Jesus, the *Mashiach* (Messiah) returns. Zechariah envisioned this consummate reconciliation of all peoples during the Messiah's rule. The characteristic of that day will be holiness. From the ordinary to the extraordinary, God will unify all in holiness. In the concluding words of Zechariah's prophecy:

> *On that day* Holy to the Lord *will be inscribed on the bells of the horses, and the cooking pots in the* Lord's *house will be like the sacred bowls in front of the altar. Every pot in Jerusalem and Judah will be holy to the* Lord *Almighty, and all who come to sacrifice will take some of the pots and cook in them (Zechariah 14:20-21).*

... *To Ponder*

• Read: John 7:1-10:21

1. The Feast of Tabernacles served as the historical backdrop for Jesus' momentous teaching recorded in John 7:1-10:21. This section contains three of the eight *"I Am"* declarations recorded solely by the apostle John. They include:

    a. *I am* the _____ (8:12 and 9:5)

    b. *I am* the _____ (10:7 and 10:8)

    c. *I am* the _____ (10:11 and 10:14)

2. Jesus likely made his pronouncement, "I am the light of the world" (8:12) on *Shemini Atzeret* (the "Eighth Day of Assembly"). He spoke these words near the treasury (8:20) in the Court of the Women. Nearby stood the massive candlesticks that were an essential part of the celebration. Jesus used the concurrent themes of darkness and light to teach eternal truths. He exposed darkness concerning:

    a. The _____ (7:19, 23)

    b. The _____ (7:47-52)

    c. The _____ (8:24)

    d. The _____ (9:24)

    e. The _____ (10:1-20)

3. The Bible uses "light" as seen by the eye and metaphorically, as reaching the mind. List who or what is associated with light in the following passages:

    a. Psalm 27:1, Isaiah 60:19 and Micah 7:8:

_____.

    b. Psalm 119:105:

_____.

    c. John 1:4-9:

_____.

    d. Luke 16:8 and John 12:36:

_____.

4. Why do you think the Bible represents Jesus as both "the Lamb of God, who takes away the sin of the world" (John 1:29) and "the good shepherd" who lays down his life for the sheep (John 10:14)? What effect does this dual metaphor have on your life?

Chapter 9

Hanukkah—
Feast of Dedication

Kindle the taper like the steadfast star
Ablaze on evening's forehead o'er the earth,
And add each night a luster till afar
An eightfold splendor shine above thy hearth.
Clash, Israel, the cymbals, touch the lyre,
Blow the brass trumpet and the
harsh-tongued horn;
Chant psalms of victory till the heart takes fire,
The Maccabean spirit leap newborn.

—Emma Lazarus

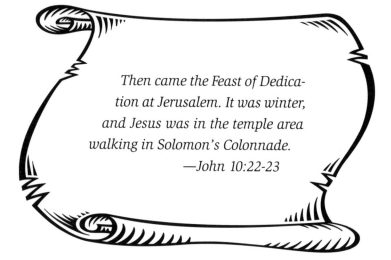

Then came the Feast of Dedication at Jerusalem. It was winter, and Jesus was in the temple area walking in Solomon's Colonnade.
—*John 10:22-23*

*H*anukkah is not one of the seven original feasts instituted by God and described in the twenty–third chapter of Leviticus. *Hanukkah* is the Hebrew word for "dedication." The Feast of Dedication is a post–Exilic feast introduced after the return from the Babylonian Exile. This was the period of the so–called "four hundred years of silence" in the time between the Old and New Testaments. We call these "silent years" because God gave no new biblical revelation during this time. Hanukkah is, however, forecast during the Babylonian Exile (Daniel 8:9-14 and 23-27). In the New Testament the feast provides the backdrop for Jesus' startling public claim to deity (John 10:22-39).

The Feast of Dedication, known today as Hanukkah, or the Festival of Lights, commences near the onset of winter on the twenty–fifth of Kislev (November–December). Throughout the eight–day celebration, the Jewish people commemorate an event often overlooked by the Gentile world—the victory of the Jews over the Syrians in 164 B.C. and the subsequent rededication of the Temple. Although not a biblical festival, it is ironically the most historically documented of all the Jewish holidays. Jewish writings have carefully recorded the historical background for the celebration (First and Second Maccabees; Josephus, *Antiquities of the Jews* 12:7; Talmud, *Shabbat* 21b).

Under the Yoke of Syria

Antiochus IV (also known as Epiphanes) reigned as King of Syria from 175-164 B.C. Known for his love of Greek culture, he despised his Jewish neighbors to the south. In 170 B.C. he launched a barbarous attack on Jerusalem, achieving a swift, decisive victory by slaughtering more than 80,000 men, women and children.

Antiochus moved quickly to obliterate all symbols of Jewish heritage and faith by replacing them with pagan counterparts. His invading legions pilfered and desecrated the Temple, destroying all copies of the Torah and converting the Temple courts into brothels. Circumcision was outlawed. Pagan priests sacrificed swine to the Greek god Zeus on the holy altar.

After six years of humiliating occupation, the Jewish people rose in revolt under the inspiration of an elderly priest named Mattathias and the virile leadership of his son, Judah. Judah was a gifted military leader who quickly earned the name, *the Maccabee*, thought to be derived from the Hebrew word *makkevet* meaning, "hammer." Under Judah's command, the Maccabees soundly defeated Antiochus in 165 B.C.

The first act of the new independent nation was to purify and rededicate the Temple. They removed the despised Greek idol of Zeus. Stone by stone, they rebuilt the altar Zerubbabel and the priest Jeshua had rebuilt three–and–a–half centuries earlier (Ezra 3:1-2). They rededicated the holy altar on Kislev 25, 165 B.C., precisely three years from its desecration.

According to Jewish tradition in the Talmud (*Shabbat* 21b), when they purified the Temple and rekindled the menorah, the Maccabees found only enough ritually pure oil to last one day. It would take eight days to produce suitable oil for the menorah. Miraculously, the single cruse of oil lasted eight days. Throughout Hanukkah, a candle is lit each day until eight burn in remembrance of this remarkable miracle.

A Startling Pronouncement

John 10:22-39 records the last time Jesus attended the Feast of Dedication, four months before his crucifixion. Two months had lapsed since his last confrontation with the authorities during the Feast of Tabernacles (John 7:1-10:21). During this brief interval Jesus traveled north to Caesarea Philippi where he instructed the disciples concerning his coming death. On a nearby mountain, probably Mount Hermon, in the presence of Peter, James and John, Jesus was transfigured (Mark 8:27-9:13). He then returned to Jerusalem with his disciples to celebrate The Feast of Dedication.

It was a cold, winter day in Jerusalem. Walking under the colonnaded, roofed porch that spanned the southern end of the Temple platform, Jesus came face to face with his adversaries. The Jewish leaders demanded an answer to the question of the day. John graphically describes the scene:

> Then came the Feast of Dedication at Jerusalem. It was winter, and Jesus was in the temple area walking in Solomon's Colonnade. The Jews gathered around him, saying, "How long will you keep us in suspense? If you are the Christ, tell us plainly" (John 10:22-24).

Jesus asserted that he had already answered that question (John 10:25), although the record suggests that only privately had he claimed to be the Messiah—to the Samaritan woman (John 4:26) and to the man born blind (9:37). His claim, Jesus continues to argue, is beyond doubt because of his *deeds* and his *words* (John 10:25-28).

Of his deeds, Jesus contended: "The miracles I do in my Father's name speak for me, but you do not believe because you are not my sheep" (John 10:25-26). He had fulfilled Isaiah's prophecy:

> Then will the eyes of the blind be opened and the ears of the deaf unstopped. Then will the lame leap like a deer, and the mute tongue shout for joy (Isaiah 35:5-6).

Of his words, Jesus cryptically noted: "My sheep listen to my voice; I know them, and they follow me. I give them eternal life, and they shall never perish; no one can snatch them out of my hand" (John 10:27-28). Then, for the first time publicly, Jesus clearly stated the fact of his divinity; his inescapable, startling conclusion; his supreme and indisputable claim: "I and the Father are one" (John 10:30)!

At this the Jewish leaders "picked up stones to stone him" (10:31). They explained that they intended to stone him "for blasphemy, because you, a mere man, claim to be God" (10:33).

A Confident Forecast

As with all other biblical feasts, Hanukkah looks forward to a greater event in the life and work of the Messiah. The Scriptures relate that another like Antiochus Epiphanes will rise:

> The man of lawlessness [will be] revealed, the man doomed to destruction. He will oppose and will exalt himself over everything that is called God or is worshiped, so that he sets himself up in God's temple, proclaiming himself to be God (2 Thessalonians 2:3-4).

When the Messiah returns in all his glory, the "man of lawlessness" will be destroyed, and Jesus Christ will "reign over the house of Jacob forever; his kingdom will never end" (Luke 1:33).

Happy Hanukkah!

The next time you hear or voice the festive greeting, "Happy Hanukkah," pause to thank the Lord for his abiding love and care. Hear afresh the reassuring words of Jesus uttered during the Feast of Dedication: "My sheep listen to my voice; I know them, and they follow me" (John 10:27).

...*To Ponder*

• Read: John 12:37-50

During the Feast of Dedication preceding his death and resurrection, Jesus declared "I and the Father are one" (John 10:30). Several months later, in the days between his triumphal entry into Jerusalem and his final Seder with his disciples, Jesus restates his claim to oneness with his Father using the central themes of the Feast of Dedication: light/darkness and deliverance/bondage.

1. John 12:44-45—Give examples in Jesus' ministry when he displayed the following divine attributes:

   a. Omnipotence ("all power")

   b. Omniscience ("all knowledge")

   c. Divine Love

   d. Divine Grace

2. John 12:46—How has Jesus brought light into a dark world? Give specific examples from his earthly life and ministry.

3. John 12:47—Deliverance from tyranny is the central theme of the Feast of Dedication. Jesus claims that he "did not come to judge the world, but to save it." How does Jesus bring deliverance without judgment?

4. John 12:49-50—How do the Father's commands lead to eternal life?

Chapter 10

Purim—Feast of Lots

Come, quaff the brimming
　　festal glass!
　　Bring forth the good old cheer!
For Esther's Feast has come at last—
　　Most gladsome in the year.

And now, when hearts beat
　　glad and free,
　　Come gather all about,
And tell once more how
　　long since, He
　　Did put our foe to rout.

Full oft has beauty ruled a land,
　　And held its sceptred sway;
Full often foiled th' avenging hand
　　And bade oppression stay.

But ne'er did beauty so avail
　　As when fair Esther's charm
'Gainst vengeful Haman did prevail
　　To 'fend the Jews from harm.

So all the dire impending woe
　　That hovered o'er their head
Did light upon their ruthless foe
　　And ruined him, instead.

And thus, throughout the ages long,
　　In every land and clime,
They chant an old thanksgiving song
　　E'er mindful of that time.

Yea, Israel's Guardian never sleeps—
　　No slumber to His eye!—
But loving watch He ever keeps
　　Upon His flock from high.
　　　　　　　　—C. David Matt

Mordecai recorded these events, and he sent letters to all the Jews throughout the provinces of King Xerxes, near and far, to have them celebrate annually the fourteenth and fifteenth days of the month of Adar as the time when the Jews got relief from their enemies, and as the month when their sorrow was turned into joy and their mourning into a day of celebration. He wrote them to observe the days as days of feasting and joy and giving presents of food to one another and gifts to the poor.

       —Esther 9:20-22

*T*hroughout the Jewish year there is no merrier occasion than Purim—known also as the Feast of Lots or the Feast of Esther. It is celebrated in the month of Adar (February–March) as a religious and secular holiday, commemorating one of the Jewish people's greatest triumphs over tyranny. Purim celebrates an enormous moral and tangible victory achieved on the eve of what was nearly annihilation.

The joyous festival venerates the deliverance of the Jews of Persia from the imminent destruction planned against them by Haman, prime minister of King Ahasuerus (Xerxes I), 485-465 B.C. The king's Jewish wife, Esther, and her cousin, Mordecai, accomplished the rescue.

Great rejoicing marks Purim. It is a day of masquerades, carnivals, parades, parties and all manner of joyous revelry—a day of uninhibited joy. As the Talmud suggests: "With the advent of Adar, joy is increased." Even in the Book of Esther, no religious ceremonies were observed. It was a time of "feasting and joy and giving presents of food to one another and gifts to the poor" (Esther 9:22).

Purim is unique among all the festivals. According to the Midrash, Purim is the only holiday that will continue in the world to come (*Yalkut Shimoni* to *Mishlei* 944). The Jewish sages also taught that "all the books of the Prophets and the Writings are destined to be abolished when the *Mashiach* (Messiah) comes, except for *Megillat Esther* (the Book of Esther). It shall endure like the five books of the Torah."[1]

The distinct significance of Purim is underscored by Jewish sages who found within it allusions to other festivals. Thus:

Purim is like Pesach—on both we emerged from bondage

---

[1] Eliyahu Kitov, *The Book of Our Heritage—The Jewish Year and its Days of Significance*, vol. 2 (Jerusalem and New York. Feldheim Publishers, 1997), 111.

to freedom.

> *Purim is like Shavuot—we accepted the Torah again on Purim.*
>
> *Purim is like Rosh Hashanna—the book of the living and the dead were opened then.*
>
> *Purim is like Yom Kippur—the generation of Purim then expiated their sins.*
>
> *Purim is like Sukkot—just as Sukkot commemorates the protection accorded us by the Divine cloud of glory in the wilderness, likewise did many non–Jews enter under the protecting wings of the Shechinah during Purim. (The reference is to Gentiles who converted to Judaism—see Esther 8:17.)*[2]

The story of Purim is recounted in the *Megillah* (the scroll of the story of Esther). It is read twice on the holiday—once at night and once during the day. The festival is also known as the Feast of Lots, since the word *Purim* means "lots." This alludes to the fact that Haman chose the day of his treachery by casting lots (Esther 3:7; 9:24, 26).

Known as "Mordecai's Day" in antiquity (2 Maccabees 15:36), Purim is celebrated on the 14th day of the lunar month of Adar (February–March)—exactly one month before Pesach (Passover). In Jerusalem and other "walled cities," the Jewish community commemorates Purim on Adar 15, one day later than the rest of the world. This is to honor the Jews in the ancient Persian capital of Shushan who did not rest from fighting until the following day (Esther 9:18). Adar 15 is therefore known as *Shushan Purim.*

The Setting

Most of the Jews remained in the 127 states of the Persian

---

[2] Ibid., 443.

King's empire, rather than return to their homeland under the leadership of Zerubbabel in 538 B.C. The Jews who stayed in Persia prospered in peace and security for more than fifty years after King Cyrus allowed them to return to Jerusalem. They became integrated, even semi–assimilated, into the Persian society. All was well—that is, until the days of King Ahasuerus and his Jewish wife, Esther.

By Esther's day the interminable seeds of anti–Semitism had again germinated. To survive, Jews like Esther and Mordecai hid their ethnic identity by taking Persian names. Esther's Hebrew name, Hadassah ("myrtle"), was fitting in light of her extraordinary beauty. Since her parents died when she was a child, her cousin, Mordecai, adopted her and cared for her as his own daughter (Esther 2:7).

Mordecai was fortunate enough to hold high office in the king's court. He had access to the palace (Esther 2:5, 11) and would often serve at the king's gate (Esther 2:21). Thus, the stage was set for an epic story of insubordination, deception, intrigue, corruption and extraordinary valor.

The Defiant Queen (Esther 1)

The biblical record notes that in the third year of King Ahasuerus' reign he held an extravagant feast that lasted six months. Persia was the world–power of the day, and the king possessed all the resources a feast of this size required. The Bible offers a vivid description of the king's magnificent palace:

> *The garden had hangings of white and blue linen, fastened with cords of white linen and purple material to silver rings on marble pillars. There were couches of gold and silver on a mosaic pavement of porphyry [stones with imbedded feld-*

spar crystals], *marble, mother–of–pearl and other costly stones* (Esther 1:6).

On the final day of the splendid feast, the inebriated King Ahasuerus ordered Queen Vashti, his wife, to appear before the princes in attendance and display her great beauty. In order to preserve her dignity, Vashti refused, and in doing so created a national crisis that threatened the status quo of Persia's male–dominated society. The king's advisers counseled that the only course of action was for the king to decree that "Vashti is never again to enter the presence of [the] king … [and] let the king give her royal position to someone else who is better than she" (Esther 1:19). The king signed the order.

The New Queen (Esther 2:1-18)

In time the king remembered Vashti and regretted his actions. Wanting a new queen, the king again followed his advisor's counsel. He launched a kingdom–wide beauty contest. The king appointed "commissioners in every province of his realm to bring all these beautiful girls into the harem at the citadel of Susa" (Esther 2:3).

One of those brought to the palace was Esther, the young Jewish woman raised by her cousin Mordecai after her parents' death. Mordecai instructed Esther not to divulge her Jewish heritage, and he kept close watch over her during the year-long beauty treatments to prepare her to meet the king. Every day Mordecai "walked back and forth near the courtyard of the harem to find out how Esther was and what was happening to her" (Esther 2:11).

Esther impressed everyone who met her, including King Ahasuerus. He was attracted to her more than any other of the women, "and she won his favor and approval … So he set a

royal crown on her head and made her queen instead of Vashti"
(Esther 2:17).

The Foiled Assassination Plot (Esther 2:19-23)

One day, while attending to his duties at the king's gate,
Mordecai overheard two of the palace guards plotting to assas-
sinate the king. Mordecai quickly reported the sinister plot to
Esther, who related the incident to the king, giving credit to
Mordecai. The king launched an investigation. The two offi-
cials were found guilty and immediately hanged.

The Villain Haman (Esther 3)

After several years, king Ahasuerus elevated Haman, a
descendant of Amalek (a traditional enemy of the Jews—see
Exodus 17:8-16; Deuteronomy 25:17-19 and 1 Samuel 15:7-9)
to the position of prime minister. Incensed by the refusal of
Mordecai to bow before him, Haman resolved not only to kill
Mordecai, but annihilate all Jews in the kingdom. Haman ob-
tained the king's authorization to exterminate all Jews in Persia on a given day, which he decided by casting lots or *purim*.
The lots determined the date of mass execution as Adar 13,
eleven months later. Word of the impending holocaust spread
rapidly throughout the empire.

Esther's Intervention (Esther 4 and 5)

When word reached Mordecai, he tore his clothes, put on
sackcloth and covered himself with ashes. He went "into the
city, wailing loudly and bitterly" (Esther 4:1). Mordecai sent
word to Esther through a trusted servant, Hathach, urging her
to intercede with the king.

Esther was understandably hesitant; such intercession could

cost her own life. Mordecai, however, urged her to accept her responsibility for her people. "If you remain silent at this time," warned Mordecai, "relief and deliverance for the Jews will arise from another place, but you and your father's family will perish. And who knows but that you have come to royal position for such a time as this" (Esther 4:14).

Persuaded by her cousin's compelling plea, Esther sought an audience with the king, who received her with amazing hospitality, offering to grant any wish "up to half the kingdom" (Esther 5:3). Esther cleverly delayed her request and instead invited the king and Haman to a banquet in her quarters.

Both men came to the banquet. During the luxuriant meal, the king again asked Esther, "Now what is your petition? It will be given you. And what is your request? Even up to half the kingdom, it will be granted" (Esther 5:6). The shrewd Esther asked only that the two return for another banquet the following night.

The Sleepless King (Esther 6)

That night, the king suffered from divinely induced insomnia. He summoned his servants and asked them to read from the royal chronicles. Perhaps he thought that a rehearsal of his impressive achievements would bring comfort and sleep. During the reading, they recited Mordecai's assistance in thwarting the attempt on the king's life.

Later that morning, Haman came into the king's court with the intent of asking for the king's approval to hang Mordecai on the gallows he had recently built. To Haman's astonishment, the king ordered him to find Mordecai and lead him on horseback throughout the city streets, proclaiming before him, "This is what is done for the man the king delights to honor!"

(Esther 6:11). Haman reluctantly followed his orders and returned to his home humiliated, and just in time for Esther's second banquet.

Esther's Banquet (Esther 7)

At the conclusion of Queen Esther's second delectable dinner, the king again pleaded with her to reveal her cherished wish. With transcendent courage, Esther finally made her petition known. She asked King Ahasuerus for the lives of her people and the death of their enemy, Haman. The king was furious. He immediately had Haman hanged on the very gallows Haman had constructed for Mordecai. "Then the king's fury subsided" (Esther 7:10).

The Right to Bear Arms (Esther 8:1-17; 9:1-16)

A fundamental problem remained. The order to annihilate the Jews had been issued with the king's own signet ring. Even the king could not revoke laws within the Medeo–Persian government. Instead, the king authorized the Jews to fight back.

When the fateful day arrived, the Jews of Persia fought for their lives. They quickly won the battle with the aid of local rulers in the outlying provinces. However, the campaign for the capital city of Shushan was fierce. The fighting there continued into the next day, Adar 15. When it was all over, the Jews of Persia had soundly defeated their enemies. A total of 75,000 perished in the provinces, 800 in Shushan. The ten sons of Haman were hanged on the gallows.

The Feast of Purim (Esther 9:17-32)

The king promoted Mordecai to prime minister, replacing

Haman. Along with Queen Esther, he instituted the Feast of Lots—Purim—as a joyful remembrance of the day of destruction that became a day of deliverance.

An Eternal Message

The significance of Purim to the Christian believer cannot be exaggerated. Christians need to be vigilant against the Hamans, Herods, Hitlers and Saddam Hussiens of history. Anti–Semitism is not a "Jewish problem." It is the infamous hatred of history, and all people are responsible to speak out and oppose it. With notable exceptions, the church and individual Christians remained silent during the Holocaust (1933-45). The silence was deafening. It remains a thunderous reminder that people of all faiths must vigorously combat hatred and prejudice.

Dr. Marvin R. Wilson, recognized leader in the dialogue between Christians and Jews, recently penned a note to this author on the subject. His penetrating, insightful plea must not be ignored:

> *Purim is a reminder that racism, bigotry and acts of hostility still exist in the world. Christians need to take a stand against those who would destroy Jews today by words and actions, for it is the Jews, more than any other people, in whose spiritual debt they stand.*

An Enduring Feast

According to Jewish tradition, only the Torah (five Books of Moses) and the Book of Esther will survive the coming of the Messiah. Tradition holds that the Book of Esther will endure because the holiness, light and truth of Purim differs from that supplied by the other festivals. The acclaimed Jewish author, Rabbi Eliyahu Kitov, reflects on the uniqueness of this book:

In what way is Purim greater than all the other holidays?

The Festivals and holidays of the Jewish year are all sanc-tified through Israel. In the days to come, when all days will be like Shabbat [the Sabbath], what need will there be for holidays? It would be like using a lamp in the middle of the day!

What can this holiness add to a world that is already filled with the light of holiness?

The light of Purim differs from that provided by the other holidays. Its source is a revelation of the holiness from above, rather than from the actions of Israel "below." This holiness will continue to shed its light even in the Messianic age …

All of the words of the Prophets were intended to strengthen the teachings of the Torah … In the World to Come, Mashgiach [Messiah] will come and he will establish the re-ligion of truth on its proper foundations.[3]

The Providence of God

While the Book of Esther does not mention God's name, we observe his power and works on every page. As the writer of Proverbs contends: "The lot is cast into the lap, but its every decision is from the LORD" (Proverbs 16:33).

---

[3] Ibid., 444-445.

... *To Ponder*

• Read: Genesis 12:2-3

Beginning with God's covenant with Abraham, God deals with humanity in the same way it treats the sons of Abraham. To curse Israel, whom God has blessed, is to place oneself in direct opposition to God.

1. What warnings concerning anti–Semitism are contained in the following verses:

    a. Exodus 23:29 _____

    b. Zechariah 2:8-9 _____

    c. Isaiah 8:10 _____

    d. Isaiah 54:17 _____

2. What blessings are promised to all nations through Israel according to the following verses?:

    a. Psalm 122:6-9 _____

    b. Acts 3:24-26 _____

    c. Galatians 3:8-9 _____

• Read: Romans 11:25-32

God has often delivered Israel in the past and in modern times, but her full deliverance awaits the return of the Deliverer—the Messiah. Only the Messiah will forever remove the yoke of Gentile oppression.

3. Who is "the deliverer [who] will come from Zion" (11:26)?

_____

4. What were the signs of his coming according to the following prophecies?:

    a. Isaiah 7:14 _____

    b. Isaiah 9:6-7 _____

    c. Isaiah 53:3, 5, 7-9, 10-12 _____

_____

Appendix

The Hebrew Calendar

Month	Length	Date	Feast
Nisan (March–April)	30 Days	Nisan 14	Passover
	Nisan 15		Unleavened Bread
	Nisan 16		Firstfruits
Iyar (April–May)	29 Days		
Sivan (May–June)	30 Days	Sivan 6	Shavuot (Pentecost)
Tammuz (June–July)	29 Days		
Av (July–August)	30 Days	Av 9	Tisha B'av
Elul (August–September)	29 Days		
Tishri (September–October)	30 Days	Tishri 1	Rosh Hashanna
		Tishri 10	Yom Kippur
		Tishri 15-21	Sukkot (Tabernacles)
Heshvan (October–November)	29 or 30 Days		
Kislev (November–December)	29 or 30 Days	Kislev 25 - Tevet 2/3	Hanukkah
Tevet (December–January)	29 Days		
Shevat (January–February)	30 Days		
Adar (February–March)	29 Days– (30 in leap yr.)	Adar 14	Purim
*Adar II (Leap Year)	29 Days	Adar II 14 (in a leap yr.)	

*To reconcile the difference between the Hebrew lunar calendar containing 354 days and the solar year comprising 365 ½ days, the Hebrew calendar consists of a nineteen–year cycle in which the third, sixth, eleventh, fourteenth, seventeenth and nineteenth years are leap years. During the Jewish leap year, one day is added to the month Adar, and a thirteenth month of 29 days, known as *Adar Sheni* ("Second Adar") or Adar II, is added to the calendar.

The Feasts of the Lord
Commanded by God in Leviticus 23

Feast	*Date*	*Messianic Relevance*
Passover (Pesach)	Nisan 14	*Passover* (Pesach) pictures the Messiah, the Passover Lamb, sacrificed for our sins (1 Corinthians 5:7)
Unleavened Bread (Hag Hamatzot)	Nisan 15-21	*Unleavened Bread* depicts a holy life—without the leaven of sin (1 Corinthians 5:8)
Firstfruits	Nisan 16	*Firstfruits* illustrates the Messiah's resurrection (1 Corinthians 15:20)
Pentecost (Shavuot)	Sivan 6	*Pentecost* (Shavuot) foreshadows the coming of the Holy Spirit (Acts 2:1-4)
Trumpets (Rosh Hashanna)	Tishri 1	*Trumpets* (Rosh Hashanna) forecasts the Messiah's triumphal return—the Rapture (1 Thessalonians 4:16-17)
Day of Atonement (Yom Kippur)	Tishri 10	*Day of Atonement* (Yom Kippur) points to the coming Messiah—The High Priest (Hebrews 9:11-14)
Tabernacles (Sukkot)	Tishri 15-21	*Tabernacles* (Sukkot) envisions the day when the Messiah consummates the messianic Kingdom (Zechariah 14:16-18)

Jesus and the Feasts of the Lord

An overwhelming majority of Jesus' ministry recorded in the Gospels (especially in the Gospel of John) takes place immediately before, during or right after the great feasts of Israel. The following events occurred in connection with a feast:

Event	Setting	Reference
Jesus comes to the Temple at twelve years of age	Passover and Unleavened Bread	Luke 2:41-50
Jesus cleanses the Temple	Passover	John 2:12-23
Nicodemus comes to Jesus at night	Passover	John 3:1-21
Jesus talks to the woman at the well and heals a royal official's son	Following the above Passover on the way back to Galilee	John 4
Jesus heals at the Pool of Bethesda and teaches about life through the Son	Unknown Feast (Likely, Rosh Hashanna)	John 5:1-47
Jesus feeds the five thousand; walks on the Sea of Galilee; teaches in the Capernaum synagogue	Passover	Matthew 14:13-36 Mark 6:30-55 Luke 9:10-17 John 6
Jesus teaches halfway through the feast (7:14) and on the last day (7:37)	Feast of Tabernacles	John 7

Event	Setting	Reference
Jesus forgives the women taken in adultery*; proclaims "I am the light of the world" (8:12; 9:5); "I am the gate for the sheep" (10:7,9) and "I am the good shepherd" (10:11, 14)	Feast of Tabernacles	John 8-10:21
Jesus proclaims: "I am God's Son" (10:36)	Feast of Dedication	John 10:22-42
Passion Week:		
The Triumphal Entry through Jesus' burial (Friday)	Passover	Matthew 21-27:61 Mark 11-15 Luke 19:28-23:56a John 12:12-19:42
Soldiers guard the tomb The women who had come from Galilee rest (Saturday)	Unleavened Bread	Matthew 27:62-66 Luke 23:56b
The Resurrection (Sunday)	Feast of Firstfruits	Matthew 28:1-15 Mark 16:1-11 Luke 24:1-49 John 20

* The earliest and most reliable manuscripts do not include John 7:53-8:11. This is no doubt a true story, although scholars continue to debate the issue. Nevertheless, the event may not have occurred during the Feast of Tabernacles that is the setting for John 7-10:21.

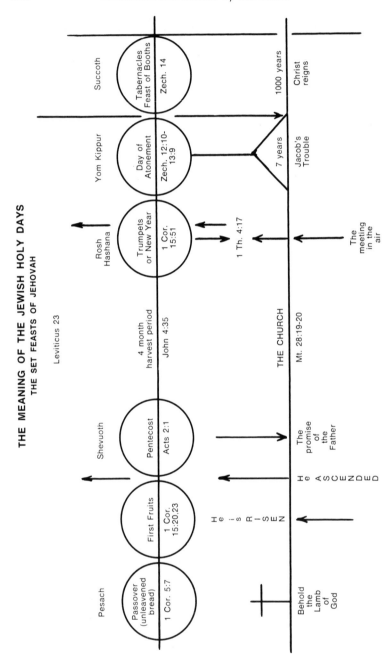

From *Israel's Holy Days in Type and Prophecy* by Daniel Fuchs: Used by permission of Loizeaux Brothers Inc., Neptune, New Jersey.

Festivals and Fast Days of the Jewish Year as Celebrated Today

Rosh Hashanna	New Year	1st of Tishri
Shabbat Shuvah	Sabbath of Return	Between Rosh Hashanna and Yom Kippur
Fast of Gedaliah	Commemorating the death of Gedaliah (appointed by the Babylonians as governor of Judah in 586 B.C.)—"the fast of the seventh month" (Zechariah 7:5; 8:19)	3rd of Tishri
Yom Kippur	Day of Atonement	10th of Tishri
Sukkot	Feast of Tabernacles	15th of Tishri (for seven days) *
Hoshanah Rabbah	Last day of Sukkot	21st of Tishri
Shemini Atzeret	Eighth Day of Assembly Observed as a one-day ** festival (two outside Israel) that immediately follows Sukkot)	22nd of Tishri *
Simchat Torah	Festival of Rejoicing with the Torah	22nd of Tishri (in Israel) 23rd of Tishri (outside Israel)
Hanukkah	Festival of Lights	25th of Kislev (for eight days)
Tu B'shevat	New Year of Trees	15th of Shevat
Purim	Feast of Lots	14th of Adar

Pesach	Passover - Festival of Matzot (Includes Feast of Unleavened Bread)	15th of Nisan (for seven days) *
Yom Hashoah	Holocaust Remembrance	27th of Nisan
Lag B'Omer	33rd Day of Omer Counting (Day of rejoicing between Passover and Pentecost—A popular day for marriages)	18th of Iyar
Shavuot	Pentecost—Feast of Weeks (50 days after Passover)	6th of Sivan *
Fast of Tammuz	Memorializes the breaching of Jerusalem's wall by Babylonians and Romans	17th of Tammuz
Tisha B'Av	Fast of the 9th of Av (The destruction of Jerusalem in 70 A.D.)	9th of Av
Elul	The month of preparation preceding the New Year	Month of Elul
Rosh Chodesh	The first of each month prompting special observance and celebration	

* The observance of these Holy Days is celebrated on one day in Israel; outside Israel, two days are customary. By the time the Jewish calendar was established in the fourth century, the custom of celebrating certain festivals two days instead of one was widely observed in many countries. This commenced when there was no fixed calendar and Jews living long distances from Israel could not be certain of the exact dates of the festivals. When the calendar was standardized, the custom remained although there was no need for an extra day. All but Reformed Jews continue this practice.

** According to 1 Kings 8:65, Solomon observed Sukkot an additional seven days. The second period of seven days is perhaps the precedent for Shemini Atzeret.

Books of the Tanach
The Hebrew Bible—Written Law

Torah
Genesis
Exodus
Leviticus
Numbers
Deuteronomy

The Early Prophets *(Early Nevi-im)*	*Latter Prophets* *(Latter Nevi-im)*		
Joshua	Isaiah	Amos	Habakkuk
Judges	Jeremiah	Obadiah	Zephaniah
1 & 2 Samuel	Ezekiel	Jonah	Haggai
1 & 2 Kings	Hosea	Micah	Zechariah
	Joel	Nahum	Malachi

The Writings *(Ketuvim)*		
Psalms	Ruth	Daniel
Proverbs	Lamentations	Ezra
Job	Ecclesiastes	Nehemiah
Song of Songs	Esther	1 & 2 Chronicles

Classic Works of Rabbinic Law, Oral Law and Commentary

The Mishnah   Compiled and edited about 200 A.D. by Yehuda Hanasi. The Mishnah contains six major divisions ("Orders") covering every aspect of Jewish Law.

The Six Orders are:

Zeraim (Seeds)	Ritual Laws, Blessings, Prayers
Moed (Festivals)	The Sabbath and all Festivals
Nashim (Women)	Marriage, Divorce, Relationships
Nezikin (Damages)	Civil and Criminal Law
Kodashim (Holy Things)	Sacrificial Laws, Temple Observance
Tohorot (Purification)	Matters of Purity and Defilement

Talmud   Compiled between 200 and 500 A.D. this classic rabbinic work was arranged according to the six orders listed above. The Talmud includes both the Mishnah and Gemara. The latter is a commentary and further explanation of the Mishnah. Rabbinic writings from the Talmud that deal only with legal matters are called *Halachah*. Pronouncements by the rabbis discussing beliefs, attitudes, stories and opinions are called *Aggadah*. Therefore, *Halachah* and *Aggadah* together provide guidelines and values by which every Jew must live.

Mishnah Torah	Compiled in the twelfth century A.D. by Maimonides, Rabbi Moses ben Maimon (Rambam). This codifies the contents of both the Written and Oral Laws with accompanying commentary.
Shulchan Aruch	Compiled in the sixteenth century A.D. by Rabbi Joseph Caro. This is the monumental code of law covering all aspects of Jewish Law applicable today to traditional Jews.
Siddur	The Daily and Sabbath Prayer Book containing all prayers for day-to-day observance. Siddurim vary from place to place and century to century, but all are based on the canonization of the liturgy by Rabban Gamliel II of the first century A.D.
Mahzor	The Siddur used for High Holiday or Festival Observances.
Haggadah	The guidebook used for the Passover (Pesach) Seder. It contains all the rituals, prayers and songs needed for the Seder—the ritual meal of Passover.

Bibliography

Ariel, Rabbi Yisrael. Translated and adapted by Chaim Richman. *The Odyssey of the Third Temple.* Jerusalem: G. Israel Publications & Productions Ltd. and the Temple Institute, 1993.

Black, Naomi, ed. *Celebration - The Book of Jewish Festivals.* New York: Jonathan David Publishers, 1989.

Doniach, N.S. *Purim - An Historical Study.* Philadelphia: The Jewish Publication Society of America, 1933.

Edersheim, Alfred. *The Temple, Its Ministry and Services as They Were at the Time of Jesus Christ.* Grand Rapids: Eerdmans, 1954.

Edidin Ben M. *Jewish Customs and Ceremonies.* New York: Hebrew Publishing Company, 1941.

Francis, William W. *The Stones Cry Out.* New York: The Salvation Army, 1993.

Fuchs, Daniel. *Israel's Holy Days in Type and Prophecy.* Neptune, New Jersey.: Loizeaux Brothers, 1985.

Galilil, Zev. Translated by Sharon Hauser. *Pesach.* Jerusalem: Avivim Publishing House.

Gaster, Theodor Herzl. *Purim and Hanukkah in Custom and Tradition.* New York: Henry Schuman Company.

Grunfeld, Dayan Dr. I. *The Sabbath.* Jerusalem and New York: Feldheim Publishers, 1981.

Hertzberg, Arthur. *Judaism.* New York: George Braziller, Inc., 1962.

Howard, Kevin and Marvin Rosenthal. *The Feasts of the Lord.* Orlando, Florida.: Zion's Hope Inc., 1997.

Josephus, Flavius. *The Complete Works of Josephus.* Translated by William Whiston. Grand Rapids: Kregel Publications, 1960.

Kitov, Eliyahu. *The Book of Our Heritage—The Jewish Year and its*

Days of Significance. 3 Vols. Translated by Nachman Bulman. Revised by Dovid Landesman. Jerusalem and New York: Feldheim Publishers, 1997.

Levitt, Zola. *The Seven Feasts of Israel.* Dallas: Zola Levitt Ministries, 1979.

Lipis, Joan R. *Celebrate Passover.* Portland, Oregon.: Purple Pomegranate Productions, 1993.

McQuaid, Elwood. *The Outpouring—Jesus and the Feasts of Israel.* Chicago: Moody Press, 1986.

Meron, Michal. *The Jewish Festivals and Holy Days.* Jaffa, Israel: The Studio in Old Jaffa, 1995.

Mishal, Miriam. Translated by Sharon Hauser. *Rosh Hashana and Yom Kippur.* Jerusalem: Avivim Publishing House.

Mishal, Miriam. Translated by Martin Friedlander and Sharon Hauser. *Purim.* Jerusalem: Avivim Publishing House.

Rosen, Moishe and Ceil Rosen. *Christ in the Passover.* Chicago: Moody Press, 1978.

Wilson, Marvin R. *Our Father Abraham—Jewish Roots of the Christian Faith.* Grand Rapids: William B. Eerdmans Publishing Company and Center for Judaic–Christian Publishing Company (Dayton, Ohio), 1989.

Yancey, Philip. *The Jesus I Never Knew.* Grand Rapids: Zondervan Publishing House, 1995.

Index

Black, James Milton 61
Blood 18, 22, 25, 49, 80, 82, 83
Boils 22
Booths 91
Bread 25, 56
Bread of Life 35
Bull, sacrificial xiv, 56, 80, 83, 92

C

Cain 70
Calendar
  Babylonian 15
  Hebrew 15, 43, 124
  lunar 16, 112, 124
  solar 16, 124
Calvary 6
Candles 5, 19
Capernaum 35, 126
Carolan, Maude 31
Chametz. *See* Leaven
Chanukah. *See* Hanukkah (Feast of Dedication)
Chief priests 47
Children of Israel. *See* Israelites
Christ. *See* Jesus Christ
Circumcision 18, 104
Court of the Women 95
Creation 67, 70
Cup of Elijah 24
Cyrus 113

D

Darkness 22
Day of Atonement. *See* Yom Kippur (Day of Atonement)
Days of Awe. *See* Rosh Hashanna (Feast of Trumpets)
Dedication, Feast of. *See* Hanukkah (Feast of Dedication)

E

Easter 43, 47, 49. *See also* Ishtar
Eden, Garden of. *See* Garden of Eden
Egypt 15, 16, 17, 21, 22, 26, 33, 56, 68, 92

N